Meditations of the Heart

Life Lessons for Renewing the Mind

Volume I

Dr. Yvonne A. Anderson

7/10

Bro Larry,

I appreciate your support of this book along with your support over the years. I am looking forward to what we will do together for the Lord.

His Love & Mine,
Dr. Anderson

Copyright © 2010 Dr. Yvonne A. Anderson

ISBN 978-1-60910-177-0

All rights reserved. No part of this publication may be reproduced, stored in a retrieval system, or transmitted in any form or by any means, electronic, mechanical, recording or otherwise, without the prior written permission of the author.

Printed in the United States of America.

BookLocker.com, Inc.
2010

This book of the law shall not depart out of your mouth, but you shall meditate on it day and night, that you may observe and do according to all that is written in it. For then you shall make your way prosperous, and then you shall deal wisely and have good success.

(Joshua 1:8)

meditate (verb) - 1. to engage in contemplation or reflection, 2. to engage in mental exercise for the purpose of reaching a heightened level of spiritual awareness. (http://m-w.com/dictionary/meditate)

Table of Contents

Preface vii

Introduction 1

"Feed My Sheep." John 21:17 32

"Put out into the deep [water], and lower your nets for a haul." Luke 5:4 64

"For God is not unjust to forget your work and labor of love which you have shown toward His name, in that you have ministered to the saints and do minister." Hebrews 6:10 118

"For everyone to whom much is given, of him shall much be required; and of him to whom men entrust much, they will require and demand all the more." Luke 12:48 170

Prayer of Salvation 215

Preface

One of the things that I was not aware of as a new believer in Christ was that there exists a "culture of silence" in the church. It has been my experience that things that happen in the everyday lives of people are not being discussed honestly and openly among "church" folk so that healing and deliverance can take place. Many times, those things are shrouded in a veil of silence.

There are people in churches all over the world who are hurting and going through trials, tests, painful experiences, crises, etc., but you would never know it because we hide behind a curtain called phoniness that offers a protective shield from those things which are painful. We, as Christians, are as adept as anyone when it comes to maintaining the phoniness facade. Week after week, we arrive at the local church dressed in our "Sunday best" accompanied by a big smile. When asked how we are doing, the response sounds something like, "Oh everything is going well. Praise the Lord!" I understand the power of positive confession or calling those things that are not as though they were (Romans 4:17), but I also understand that sometimes it becomes necessary to share what's going on on the inside with others. Sometimes, you just need to be "real." I am not

Life Lessons for Renewing the Mind - Volume I

advocating sharing your situation or circumstance with anyone who will listen, but rather share it with a spiritually mature, trustworthy Christian who can offer you effective prayer, godly wisdom, and godly counsel.

Do you ever feel like you are the only person going through a particular test or trial? Did you ever wonder if there were any others out there who could identify with your situation? I have often felt this way, and it was not until I began to write this book, and allowed others to read it, that I came upon individuals who had had the same or similar experiences. The irony is that we were having some of the same issues; yet, we had never discussed them with one another. We just kept them under lock and key, tucked safely away, inside the phoniness box.

In hindsight, I have to admit that I had assimilated into the "culture of silence" in the church rather covertly. I can't even pinpoint when it happened, but I found myself a part of a socially acceptable more, within the church, that I didn't even know existed. I found myself imitating what others were doing, or should I say "not doing?"

I began to forget that each week I was coming into contact, in the church, with "real people" who had "real problems" that required "real solutions," and I was one of them. I entertained the idea that things were going well for others due to their outward appearance and their response to my inquiry about their welfare. Can you say, "Don't judge a book by its cover?" I was satisfied with this mindset. Can I be real with you and talk about my issue for a minute?

My assignment, in this endeavor, is to share my real-life, everyday experiences with others. Some will identify with the same and/or similar situations while others will locate themselves immediately and unequivocally. My hope is that my transparency in breaking the "culture of silence" will help someone else get delivered. It's just that simple. Throughout the writing of this work, I have tried to write in love under the leadership and guidance of the Holy Spirit.

With this goal in mind, I will have completed my assignment as unto the Lord, and I am satisfied.

<u>Meditations of the Heart, Life Lessons for Renewing the Mind: Volume 1</u> has been written as an outgrowth of various life experiences. A scripture that has sustained, supported, rebuked, corrected, renewed, changed, inspired, delivered, and/or strengthened my walk with God supports each experience. My prayer for you is that you will allow the Spirit of the living God to minister to your heart as you read. As a result, I believe your mind will be changed and/or renewed about the matter unswervingly.

Life Lessons for Renewing the Mind - Volume I

Remember that in order to make your way prosperous, you must meditate on the Word day and night and do all that is written in it (Joshua 1:8). As you read, open your Bible. Study the scriptures that are found in the text for yourself. Get ready to receive. God is always speaking! He who has ears, let him hear what the Spirit of the Lord is saying (Matthew 13:9).

Please note that all biblical references that appear in their full context have been taken from the amplified version of the Bible unless otherwise indicated.

Introduction

Your thinking determines your decisions.
Your decisions determine your actions.
Your actions determine your habits.
Your habits determine your character.
Your character determines your destiny.
<u>Secrets of the Millionaire Mind</u>,
T. Harv Eker, 2005

Divine destiny is the reason that you and I are here. God has a divine destiny for each of us to fulfill. It is a destiny that has been created by design. If you read the statements above again, you will discover that your thinking starts the process of reaching that destiny. Only when you and I, as believers, meditate day in and day out upon the Word of God can we begin the process of renewing the mind or changing the way we think. By becoming a Christian, you and I have made a quality decision to become a new creation "in Christ." The old previous moral and spiritual condition has passed away. Behold, the fresh and the new have come (2 Corinthians 5:17)! The "newness" the Bible refers to includes the mind, but the process is neither something that takes place by osmosis, nor does it take place overnight. In other words, renewing the mind is an ongoing process that requires time, work, and diligence.

There was a time when each of us was "in the world," and we thought and acted like the world. As members of the Body of Christ, we must now accept the responsibility for aligning our thinking and thought processes with the Word of God if we are to ever have and enjoy the life Jesus died to give us. The Bible tells us in Romans 12:2:

> Do not be conformed to this world (this age), [fashioned after and adapted to its external, superficial customs], but be transformed (changed) by the (entire) renewal of your mind [by its new ideals and its new attitude], so that you may prove [for yourselves] what is the good and acceptable will of God, even the thing which is good and acceptable and perfect [in His sight for you].

The alignment of our thinking and thought processes with the Word of God must penetrate the psyche to the point of <u>total</u> and <u>complete</u> saturation. In time, new thought processes will begin to take over our minds at both the conscious and subconscious levels. Worldly or carnal responses to situations and circumstances, along with old decision making habits, will begin to be replaced by godly thoughts and godly habits. These new thought patterns and habits will influence and determine our character, which then determines our destiny. Divine destiny is why we are here. Are you starting to get the picture?

The Bible tells us in the book of Genesis (1:26) that we have been made in His likeness and in His image. I like to think of myself as "Handmade;" in which case, I, along withe every other human being, have an innate ability to think like and act like my heavenly Father. In other words, we come well equipped because the spiritual genetics are already there when we are born into this world.

We were created by God in His image and likeness (Genesis 1:26). Remember? If God is a spirit (John 4:26), then we are spirits first and foremost, even though we have a soul that lives in a human body. You and I have the spiritual genetics of our Father and Creator just as we have the genetics of our human parents. When we realize this, we can learn to identify and cast aside the excuses that are sometimes used to justify ungodly thoughts and actions that go against or are contrary to the Word of God. Spiritual genetics suggest that we come into the world inherently "well-equipped." No excuses.

You might ask, "If I have this innate ability to be like my heavenly Father, why doesn't it just manifest or show itself over time?" I think, to some extent, it does manifest itself. It may go unnoticed and without any conscious effort on our part, but I believe that the manifestations do take place in our lives. We can't help it. We are predisposed to act like our Father. Take a moment and think about the origins of things like acts of kindness, or showing love and compassion to others when they are hurting, or patting someone on the back, etc. From whom do these kinds of behaviors originate? God is the Originator, and there is no other. He is good, and He is love, but He doesn't stop there. He always wants to bring His children to a much deeper level in Him, which is one of the reasons why He has commanded us to renew our minds with His Word. A renewed mind will solicit an increase in the types of behaviors that I just described.

Now you are aware that you have a divine calling, so let's talk for a moment about life before the salvation found in Jesus Christ. Many of us have long been conditioned to think and act like "the world." When I refer to "the world," I mean the things in this natural realm that oppose or are contrary to the Word of God. Because you and I have been born into this world under the umbrella of the sin of Adam and Eve, the processes that have shaped our thinking and behaviors were years in the making, and they will require time to reshape and refine, and in some cases, completely undo. Is light dawning?

Mind renewal will require a relearning of many of the things we have learned throughout our lives, but be encouraged because we <u>can</u> do all things through Christ who strengthens us (Philippians 4:13). In other words, you and I don't have to do it alone. Jesus has made a promise and a commitment to being our Helper. I really like the amplified version of Philippians 4:13 which says:

> I have strength for all things in Christ who empowers me [I am ready for anything and equal to anything through Him who infuses inner strength into me; I am self-sufficient in Christ's sufficiency].

This verse is saturated with potential for the believer who realizes it is impossible to do anything without Him, but who is wise enough to receive the help He has made available to him.

Renewing the mind is a lifelong process. It is going to require a steadfast commitment from every individual who desires to obey the Word of God. The good news is that the process is not one-sided. God will and has continually committed Himself to helping us with mind renewal whether we commit or not. Even during the times when we lack conviction, slack off, and even falter in doing our part, His commitment to us stands. He promises that He is the God who doesn't change. He is the same yesterday, today, and forever more (Hebrews 13:8). This is a really good time and place to shout about the faithfulness of our God! I have come to a place in my life where I am extremely appreciative of His faithfulness because no matter what, it's always there. It's steadfast, and it's unconditional.

Commitment opens the door to the power of God to work in our lives. This same power allows you and me to operate in the Kingdom of God system and to have the benefit of the manifestations of His promises. As part of His commitment, our Heavenly Father is ready, willing, and able to assist us whenever and wherever we are in the process. That's terrific news!

Life Lessons for Renewing the Mind - Volume I

  To assist in our commitment, the Lord has made a number of helpful tools available to His children, but "knowing" tools have been made available and actually making use of them are two different things. For example, tools lying in a tool shed can be of no assistance to my becoming a successful gardener. They can only assist me when I take them out and make use of them in the gardening process. Please keep in mind; however, proper use is always essential.

  One of the greatest God-given tools is the Bible, but a Bible that is only opened on Sundays, or one that gathers dust in the trunk of the car from one week to the next, or one used only to hold family records is essentially rendered an ineffective, nonproductive tool to the "would be" user. Without a doubt, the Bible has the potential to show you and me how to be empowered, but again, just knowing about and properly using that knowledge are two entirely different things. I would like to take this point a few steps further and stress to you that as you acquire the knowledge, make sure you understand it (Proverbs 4:5). Opening your Bible is a good start, but it is essential that you understand and search out what you read in order to augment your understanding. "It is the glory of God to conceal a thing, but the glory of kings is to search it out" (Proverbs 25:2). Once you understand the knowledge, put it into action. Don't just walk around with a bunch of "head knowledge" that doesn't do anyone any good.

God has given His Body the fivefold ministry gifts to train up the saints to do the work of the ministry (Ephesians 4:11-12). That's why it is so important to be connected to the "right" Bible-based ministry that God has chosen for you. Did you know that you and I don't choose our church? We think we do, but ultimately God chooses it for us. I did not know that for the longest time, but spiritual growth and maturity has shown me this is the case. Furthermore, as believers, we want to be able to recognize the voice of God. Knowing and understanding His Word will help us to do that because God always speaks in line with

His Word. You and I won't know when He's speaking if we don't know and understand what His Word says. This is where a good Bible-based church plays an essential role in the nourishment and growth of the spiritual man.

Praise God that we don't have to remain in the darkness of an old, unrenewed mind any longer. For the benefit of those who are not as mature in age, perhaps as others, please understand that physical age is <u>not</u> a factor here. It has no bearing on "when" the process of renewing the mind begins in a life. God knows exactly when our divine appointment with His destiny for our lives will take place. His timing is always perfect! In other words, when we make a quality decision to come out of darkness into the marvelous light by receiving Jesus Christ as Lord and Savior and allow Him to begin to line up our thinking with His Word, God will meet us right where, when, and how we are. In addition, He will provide the grace to do whatever is necessary to become that "new creature" that will lift Him up in our lives so that all men will be drawn to Him (John 12:32).

The process of "becoming" Christlike will provide the believer with testimony after testimony in which God will have taken us from glory to glory and from faith to faith. I have to caution you here. Oftentimes, we want to bypass the process for the progress. God desires to develop spiritual fruit in each and every one of us. It's a process that takes time. He also desires to remove or cut off those things that are not bearing "good" fruit. This too, is a process that takes time. God wants to put you and me in the place that He desires, in that place of divine destiny where our godlike character will sustain us and not bring a reproach to the name of the Lord. No matter where you are in the process, I encourage you to keep moving forward!

Experience in God will give you and I a testimony, and He wants us to share our experiences of His goodness with others so they too will be encouraged, delivered, and/or set free from bondage. Again, this sentiment has been one of the motivations for writing this book. The Word of God says we overcome by the blood of the Lamb and the Word of our testimony (Revelation 12:11).

Have I got your attention? Shall we get started? What do we need to do? Let me respond, first of all, by assuring you that the God we serve is not complicated in that He makes Himself (His Word) "whosoever will" friendly. Consider yourself a "whosoever."

The first step in the process of renewing the mind is to recognize and receive the fact that God has commanded each of us to be constantly renewed in our minds. The operative words here are commanded and constantly. Ephesians 4:22-24 states:

Strip yourselves of your former nature [put off and discard your old unrenewed self] which characterized your previous manner of life and becomes corrupt through lusts and desires that spring from delusion; And be constantly renewed in the spirit of your mind [having a fresh mental and spiritual attitude]; And put on the new nature (the regenerate self) created in God's image, [Godlike] in true righteousness and holiness.

You have already taken a step towards recognition and receiving the commandment of God, relative to mind renewal, in that you have this book in your hand. I believe that God will not only honor your effort in purchasing and reading the book, but I believe He will speak to your heart throughout our journey together. I declare and decree the anointing that is contained within these pages will strip every yoke, remove every burden, and break every bondage that has ever hindered you in the area of mind renewal, in Jesus' name. Be encouraged! Press in! Press on!

The second step in the process of renewing the mind is to make a quality decision to renew it. Only you can decide. Our Father is a gentleman, and He will never force any of His children to make this or any other decision, but He is always motivating and encouraging us, through His promises, to choose the higher, more excellent way. The Book of Job (36:11) expresses this idea very plainly: "If they obey and serve Him, they shall spend their days in prosperity and their years in pleasantness and joy."

I want to live the "good life" in the land of the living where there is pleasantness and joy. I am sure you do too. The only way to do that is by deciding through personal choice to live the godly kind of life. If you have not had the experience, I encourage you with all of my heart to "taste and see that the Lord is good. Blessed [happy, fortunate, to be envied) is the man who trusts and takes refuge in Him" (Psalm 34:8).

You can make a quality decision right now. Why wait? What's been holding you back? A challenging situation and/or circumstance? As you will discover in the testimonies that follow, I have been there and done that. When faced with making a quality decision, Joshua (24:15) responded:

And if it seems evil to you to serve the Lord, choose for yourselves this day whom you will serve, whether the gods which your father served on the other side of the river, or the gods of the Amorites, in whose land you dwell, but as for me and my house, we will serve the Lord.

David, the Psalmist, understood the importance of quality decision-making as well: "I have chosen the way of truth and faithfulness, Your ordinances have I set before me" (Psalm 119:30). "Let Your hand be ready to help me, for I have chosen Your precepts" (Psalm 119:173).

Pick up your Bible and begin to read about the goodness of God in the lives of His people, and while you are reading, remember that He is the same yesterday, today, and forevermore (Hebrews 13:8).

That means that even in the modern day in which we live, God is still in the goodness business, especially when it comes to His children. If you have children, then you know how He feels about His offspring.

The final step in renewing the mind is to constantly and consistently meditate on the Word of God. You might ask, "Isn't that something you do when perhaps you are participating in something like a yoga class?" That may very well be the case, but that's not the type of meditation to which I am referring.

According to Webster (1977), to meditate means to exercise the mind in contemplation or thought, to plan mentally, to design, to reflect, to mutter, to put to word, to muse over, to practice beforehand, to actualize in the realm of the Spirit, etc.

"The world" has taught and/or conditioned you and me, whether we realize it or not, to "meditate," especially during a crisis. Selah! Pause and think about that. When a situation comes up in our lives, how do many of us respond? We think about it, and we talk about it constantly. We wring our hands over it and pace back and forth as if engaging in these behaviors will resolve the problem. We may even engage in conversation with others where we rehearse the situation repeatedly, and for what purpose? It's called worry, and it's <u>always</u> counterproductive. The Bible says there is no man, who by worrying, will add one moment to his life; therefore, we should seek first the Kingdom of God (Matthew 6: 31-33) and His righteousness, His way of doing and being right, before we do anything else. It goes on to state, "Sufficient for the day is its own trouble" (34).

Worrying will consume the mind to the point where it can become difficult to function in everyday life because the problem has become so amplified, at least mentally, that it consumes every waking thought. In some cases, you can't eat, or think, or even sleep. Ever been there? I have, and in the end, it was a complete waste of my time, effort, and energy, and the problem still existed.

Are you starting to get the picture? Does any of this sound familiar? Do you know what I've discovered? In the aftermath of all of my attempts at mental problem solving, the problem did not decrease nor did it go away. Meditating on it stole away precious time. That was time that I could have spent resting in the peace of God and trusting in His Word, even in the midst of feeling helpless to enact a solution to the problem. The Bible tells us in Psalm 116:7, "Return to your rest, O my soul, for the Lord has dealt bountifully with you." It boggles my mind to think that God has an answer for <u>all</u> of our concerns in His Word. He placed them in the sixty-six books of our covenant, called the Bible, before you and I were ever born. Selah! Pause and think about that. He gives us a double assurance by stating, "It shall be that before they call, I will answer; and while they are yet speaking, I will hear" (Isaiah 65:24). We are "they."

Let's take a look at meditation from the productive perspective. Can you imagine how spiritually powerful you and I could become if we got a revelation about the profit to be gained from investing time in reading, studying, speaking, discussing, and learning about the Word of God? When a situation arises, and it will, wouldn't it be a refreshing change if our minds defaulted to what the Word of God has to say about it and then moved on to our hearts, emotions, lips, and behavior? Can you imagine the peace that would come over you and me as we would begin to be ushered into the rest of the Word of God? "For we, who have believed, shall enter that rest" (Hebrews 4:3). The book of Hebrews goes on to state, "There remains therefore a rest for the people of God. For he who has entered His rest has himself also ceased from his works as God did from His" (Hebrews 4:9-10). I want you to notice the word "cease" in that scripture. It tells us that we can cease or stop engaging in counterproductive behaviors. God has our backs. He holds us in the palm of His hand from which no one can pluck us (John 10:28). Hallelujah!

Let me assure you that the "Hebrews" kind of peace, confidence, assurance, and ultimately deliverance will come only by meditating on the Word of God constantly. I am not just referring to our prayer time. God wants to be a part of our everyday lives from sunup to sundown. He wants to be involved in every aspect of it. He desires that you and I have an ongoing living daily connection with Him.

How many years did I limit God's involvement in my life to a Sunday morning church service or to my "alloted" prayer time? I didn't see the need, nor did I understand the necessity of having Him totally and completely involved in my life, not only daily, but all day long. I thought I was smart enough to run my own life. Wrong! One day, I received some understanding from the Bible, which says that apart from Him, I can do nothing (John 15:5).

I can remember calling upon God and wanting Him involved in my life primarily when faced with a crisis. Is this ringing any bells for you? Do you know how hard it is to go before the Lord, or anybody else for that matter, and ask for help when you haven't exactly invested any quality time in cultivating that relationship? On top of that, you may sometimes feel guilt and condemnation because you know that you haven't done everything "right." Shake it off! There's good news as the apostle Paul explains in 2 Corinthians 12:9:

But He said to me, My grace (My favor and lovingkindness and mercy) is enough for you [sufficient against any danger and enables you to bear the trouble manfully]; for My strength and power are made perfect (fulfilled and completed) and show themselves most effective in [your] weakness. Therefore, I will all the more gladly glory in my weaknesses and infirmities, that the strength and power of Christ (the Messiah) may rest (yes, may pitch a tent over and dwell) upon me!

I thank God that He was and still is patient enough to wait for me as I come farther and farther out of the darkness and into His marvelous light through my relationship with His Son, Jesus. By no means have I arrived, and as I stated earlier, the process of renewing the mind is an ongoing one for every believer. My heart's desire is to help others and to share with them what my Father has done for me;

thereby, making an impact in their lives that will have a lifelong effect. Some of us will plant, others will water, but God will bring forth the increase [into the lives of His people] (1 Corinthians 3:6).

It is time for the Word of my testimony!

"Feed My Sheep." John 21:17

If we begin at verse 15 of the book of John, chapter 21, we will find that Jesus is asking Peter if he loves Him more than the others. Peter responds in the affirmative. Jesus then tells Peter to feed His lambs. In the sixteenth verse, Jesus asks Peter the same question again to which he, for the second time, responds in the affirmative. Once again, Jesus tells Peter to tend or shepherd His sheep. In the seventeenth verse, the same question is asked of Peter for the third time. Jesus asks:

Simon, son of John, do you love Me [with a deep, instinctive, personal affection for Me, as a close friend]? Peter was grieved (was saddened and hurt) that He should ask him the third time, Do you love Me? And he said to Him, Lord you know everything, You know that I love You [that I have a deep, instinctive, personal affection for You, as a close friend]. Jesus said to him feed My sheep. (John 21:17)

Life Lesson

I love to run, not only to stay in shape, but also to clear my mind. I think the Lord has given me both the desire and the motivation to run because it is one of the few times in my life when my mouth is completely closed, and my ears are completely open. It is a little difficult to inhale and talk at the same time, and I believe the Lord uses this time to get a word in edgewise. Can I get a witness? By nature, I am a talker, but that's another book. Running gives me the opportunity to improve my listening skills. Not only can I hear others talking, but I tend to hear God more clearly. Imagine hearing God more clearly. What a thought!

One particular day, I was out on the track running. As I was rounding the curve, I heard the Lord ask me if I loved Him. I had been meditating on John 21:17, and I remembered how Peter responded. I said, "Lord, You know all things. You know that I love You," and I meant it. He said, "Then get up. I have need of you!" I felt a little like Peter in that the Lord knows all things. Why couldn't He just search my heart and see that it was full of love for Him? He knew I had a willing and obedient heart. I had made up my mind I was going to serve Him long before He asked me that question. Since My Father knows all things, He knew what my answer would be in advance; but alas, He always has the bigger picture in mind. He always has a plan and a purpose.

One of the things I have discovered about God is that oftentimes when He brings something to our attention, it is not for His sake but for ours and/or someone else's sake. Of course, He already knew I loved Him, but there were some things I still had not understood about my love for Him. He desired that I begin to examine just how much and in what ways I loved Him. He was asking me to go beyond the words in loving Him and in loving others. He was helping me to understand that the love of God should have manifestation and be more than just "lip service." It should not be, at any time, relegated to empty rhetoric that is devoid of power and purpose.

As children who have been fashioned in the image of their Father, it is imperative that we make it a point to discover who we are in Christ and what we have been birthed to do individually and collectively. It takes some of us a while to understand and accept the fact that our purpose for existing on planet earth doesn't even come close to just "taking up space" and going through the daily exercise of inhaling and exhaling.

As members of the Body of Christ, it is critical to our ability to be effective for the Kingdom of God that we realize at some point, our new life in Him should go beyond the wearing of the title of "Christian" on our foreheads because of the free gift of salvation, or faithfully attending a Sunday morning church service, or wearing a Jesus pin, or even having just the right Christian response on our lips ("Praise the Lord," "Hallelujah" etc.). I am not saying any of these things are wrong. I do all of them. What I am saying is that there is so much more to living the Christian life. There has to be more depth to you and me than just the "appearance" of spiritual fruit. Where there are leaves, there should be fruit.

The kinds of things I mentioned in the paragraph above only scratch the surface of a sincere and deeper walk with God. Allow me to reiterate that they are all "good" things, but God has called each of us to a deeper place in Him that will only come as we draw nearer to Him. In return, He has promised to draw nearer to us (James 4:8).

Are you starting to get the picture? There is a responsibility associated with being a member of the Body of Christ, and we are supposed to take it seriously. I have often heard it said that God doesn't save us just for ourselves. At the most elementary level, He saves us to help others. I believe this to be the "true" essence of salvation. In other words, it's not about you or me. It's about building the Kingdom of God. How do we do that? We become trained and/or equipped by way of the doma gifts, also called the fivefold ministry gifts, to do the work of the ministry (to and for others). According to Ephesians 4:11, those gifts include the apostles, the prophets, the evangelists, the shepherds, and the teachers.

The Lord was asking me if I loved Him enough to do what He was telling me to do: love Him and love others. This is the work of the ministry of Jesus. He has commanded:

> You shall love the Lord your God with all your heart and with all your soul and with all your mind (intellect). This is the great (most important, principal) and first commandment. And a second is like it. You shall love your neighbor as [you do] yourself. (Matthew 22:37-38)

Two simple commandments........ How hard can they be? How often do we, as believers, become so satisfied and so complacent in our own Christianity that we fail to go beyond our own salvation? Often, especially when we are young and inexperienced in the Lord, "loving the Lord" doesn't go beyond our heads or our hearts, which can be stifling to our ability to mature in the things of God and to reach out to others. Additionally, many Christians may feel the job or the responsibility of "feeding the sheep" belongs to the local pastor. It does, but it is also the responsibility of every believer. The Bible tells us:

> And He said to them, Go into all the world and preach and publish openly the good news (the Gospel) to every creature [of the whole human race]. (Mark 16:15)

God has not changed His mind about His commandments. He is the same yesterday, today, and forevermore (Hebrews 13:8). The same commandments He gave to Jesus Christ, His Son, He has also given to every believer. If you will read the opening scripture once again, you will notice it doesn't contain any fine print that states it is applicable to pastors only. Every believer or Christian, that's you and me, has his or her own pulpit. That pulpit may not be in the local church, but each one of us has our own circle of influence where there are people who look to us for leadership and/or guidance. They are God's sheep, and sheep must be fed in order to live. For example, if you have children, you know that they will look to you for leadership and guidance as they grow and mature. They are also God's sheep, and again, sheep have to be tended and fed to live.

I find it extremely interesting that Jesus tells Peter to feed His lambs in one instance, and in another, He says to feed His sheep. Did you notice that? Go back and read it again. Lambs are young sheep. Some people with whom we come into contact, will be very young and tender in the Lord while others will have some level of spiritual maturity. Regardless of individual levels, we have all been called to minister to the sheep, and sheep beget sheep.

Can you begin to see the importance of meditating on God's Word in an effort to renew your mind? You can't share with others that which you do not know. You can "do better" only when you "know better," and God has made several provisions to assist His children in this area. I mentioned the doma gifts earlier; one of which is the gift of the local pastor. One of his or her jobs is to train up the sheep to go out and minister to other sheep. I will say it again. Sheep beget sheep. That's doing the work of the ministry. That's doing the work of Jesus' ministry. All of a sudden, the big picture isn't about you or me. Then again, it never was. It's about the will of the Father for our lives individually and collectively that has to be executed because someone is waiting for what you and I have to give. That was a sobering revelation for me.

When I began to understand this revelation, I had to seriously examine my love for the Lord. How could I say I loved Him if I wasn't willing to love others enough to feed them? Jesus tells us the person who loves Him will keep His two most important commandments. He says in John 14:21:

> The person who has My commandments and keeps them is the one who [really] loves Me; and whoever [really] loves Me will be loved by My Father, and I [too] will love him and will show (reveal, manifest) Myself to him. [I will let Myself be clearly seen by him and make Myself real to him].

Knowing and understanding that you and I have been commanded to love others is part of the process of renewing the mind. I can guarantee you God will inevitably bring people across your path who will challenge your ability to love them; in which case, you and I have to be ready to respond to that person or persons in a way that glorifies God. New behaviors start with new thoughts that line up with the Word of God. When we have meditated consistently and purposefully on that Word, day and night, our subconscious mind will automatically kick in to assist us in the kind of higher, more excellent responses that say, "Yes Lord, I love You, and I will love my neighbor as I love myself."

I don't want to give you the impression that loving people is easy in any way, shape, or form. It isn't. As a matter of fact, I can guarantee you that loving unlovely people is quite challenging. Learning to love them will stretch and mature you if you cooperate with God. "If" is the operative word here because it involves a personal choice to allow God to have His way.

I once thought I could pick and choose who I would love. Not! I found out later that if I was planning to operate successfully in the Kingdom of God system, being selective when it comes to loving others was not an option. It was, and still is, a command.

In the beginning, God loved us so much that He sent His only Son to die for us (John 3:16). His love continues here and now. He expects it to come up and out of His children each day especially since it's been shed or poured out in our hearts through the Holy Spirit who has been given to us (Romans 5:5). First John 4 further emphasizes the point by stating, "Beloved, if God loved us so [very much], we also ought to love one another." I just love the fact that God, like any good teacher, has modeled the appropriate behavior. He has not asked us to do anything He has not been willing to do Himself. He leads us by example constantly. Additionally, He has removed the possibility of any confusion by plainly stating in His Word, more than once, what we have been commanded to do. If that isn't enough, He asks us how we can love

Him whom we have never seen, yet not love our brother whom we see every day (1 John 4:20). Hmm.

You might say the word "commanded" sounds a little strong, and that may be, but have you ever stopped to give thought to the fact that the creator of a thing has the right to decide "how" the creation should operate? We are all, the saved and the unsaved, God's creation. With that in mind, it would seem that He knows what's best for us: the creation; however, He never forces His will upon us. He's always a gentleman. He wants us to make a quality decision to choose to live our lives according to His operation manual: the Bible.

I loved God, or so I thought. The Bible tells us the person who does not love doesn't know God because God is love (1 John 4:8). At that time, you wouldn't have been able to convince me that I couldn't have known God just because I wasn't loving His people. I did love Him, but I still had a long way to go in my relationship with Him and with His people. The fruit of love needed major development in my life.

For example, in my ignorance about the command to love others, I would "cut people off at the knees" (not literally). What I mean is that I would allow a spirit of offense to keep me from interacting with you ever again. You were crossed off of my list, if you will.

You were "X ed." I wasn't vindictive in the aftermath, but I wasn't going to love you either. Big mistake!

Then, I had a limited understanding of the love of God. Praise Him that He eventually brought me to a place where I was able to renew my mind on the subject of loving Him and others. At that point, I became responsible for what I had heard. God got right in my face and asked me if was I going to do things His way or my way. I chose to do things His way, the higher more excellent way. I could have chosen to go the other way, but I guarantee you my life would have been miserable. I do want to clarify that "loving others," especially those who have hurt you, does not mean that you have to reestablish a relationship with them, but you do have to love and forgive them. Besides, unforgiveness keeps you and I in bondage not the other person. Give yourself the gift of forgiveness by releasing those who have hurt you.

People are everywhere you go. Have you noticed that? You and I have to come into contact with them in the course of our everyday lives. There is no way a person can live in a bubble, no matter how hard s/he may try. Besides, who would want to live like that? Is that really existing? I don't think so.

Because I was saved, I would have still gone to heaven, but I would never have experienced the life, here on earth, that Jesus died to give me. His Word says He came so you and I can have and enjoy life in abundance to the full and until it overflows (John 10:10). You can't live an abundant life living in a bubble that separates you from people. There's no overflow in that because it's limited to just you. I think Barbara Streisand spoke profoundly as well as prophetically when she sang the song "People." I encourage you to research the words to the song. I did, and they really ministered to me in a way that gave them strong implications for my life and ministry.

Relationships are so vital and so precious. Don't take them for granted. We all have the need to interact with others; but sometimes, we go behind that veil of phoniness that protects our pride and separates us from others; in which case, you and I run the risk of holding others responsible for information about ourselves that we have neglected to openly and honestly share with them. It's unfair, and it's out of balance.

Did you know you and I have an inherent need to love each other? It might sound a little corny, but it's true. How do I know? Because we have been made in the image and likeness of God (Genesis 1:26), and God is love (1 John 4:8). God loves people. He says so throughout His Word. That's how I know.

If you think you have never experienced the love of God, I invite you to begin to take an inventory of your life. Think about all the times God has manifested His love for you through other people. Think about all the times He protected you from hurt, harm, and danger. Think about all the times when you received preferential treatment over others, and you chalked it up to "a lucky day." That was God's favor working on your behalf. There is no such thing as luck, so begin to count your blessings.

If that's not enough to show you His love is steadfast and unchanging towards you, make it a goal of yours right now to get to know Him more intimately. Spend more time cultivating your relationship with Him through prayer, Bible study, reading His Word, and talking to Him just like you would any other person. God has always been there for you and for me, and He will continue to be there. I promise you He will show you just how amazing His love really is. It's steadfast. It's unchanging! It's faithful! It's awesome!

We were talking about hiding our needs. A "culture of silence" will keep our needs hidden unless we allow the Lord to help us, through the vehicle of His love, to reach out to others. Sometimes, the only way to break out of that kind of bondage is to become transparent, which means there is a risk involved, but He has promised never to leave us or forsake us (Hebrews 13:5) no matter what. I invite you to allow God to deliver you from all that's been "hidden." It's bondage. Allow Him to cleanse your heart so He can replace it with His heart: a heart that's full of love for Him and for His creation, a heart that is not being smothered by offense, hurt, and unforgiveness.

As you know, children tend to be immature in certain areas of their lives because they have not been taught the proper way to do things. Instruction, assistance, and guidance therefore are imperative in their formative years. This same scenario can be applied to you and me as children of God. We come into the world separated from Him by sin, but He has loved us enough to give us the free gift of salvation through His Son Jesus Christ. Once we make a choice to receive Jesus, we become new babes, or should I say "lambs," in Christ? Just like children in the natural must be assisted in the maturation process, so too, must the Christian. You will notice I did not say "the baby" Christian because as long as we live on this earth and inhabit bodies made of flesh, you and I will continue to need and require, as a vital necessity, assistance, guidance, and instruction from our Heavenly Father.

The process of loving people cannot be limited to just the words. It involves so much more. I am not saying that the words, "I love you" are meaningless, but they become empty rhetoric when they are not accompanied by the appropriate godly behaviors to support them. We have all heard the saying, "Actions speak louder than words." Godly behaviors, like all other behaviors both good and bad, not only have to be learned, but they must be practiced. Yes, I said "practiced." The real test lies in whether or not we are willing to practice them on the unlovely.

Love can manifest itself in something as simple as a "hello" or a smile as you pass by another person. It might be a word of encouragement or a listening ear or even a genuine hug. It doesn't have to be a full blown sermon. God will use us anywhere and at any time, if we will make ourselves available and sensitive to the leading of His Holy Spirit. Remember that God and His Word are "user friendly" for whosoever will use it.

OK, so have I been able to master the "loving others" commandment? Have I arrived? No, and I acknowledge that I will forever continue in the process, but I thank God I am not where I used to be in it. My intention is to keep moving forward in God. He is my only assurance of success.

I thank God that He has renewed my mind in the area of loving Him and others, but I have to tell you mind renewal has been neither a solo or single event. Yes, I understand the "need" to love others, but I also understand that I can't do that alone. Many times, my flesh wants to get into the driver's seat of my life and dictate my actions, but that's when I have to allow the Word of God, on which I have meditated, to rise within me to overtake and subdue my fleshly nature. Am I always successful? No, which is why I have to acknowledge that I need the Lord. I depend upon Him as a vital necessity in my life. He is my Father, and I am His child; therefore, I can boldly go to His throne and ask for help during those times when I feel weak. There's no shame in that. Besides, He knows all things, so it's pointless for me to try to hide anything from Him.

You might ask, "Has the commission changed in light of my shortcomings?" No. I am still a child of the King. I am still the apple of His eye and the beat of His heart. He still loves me with the same love with which He has loved my Jesus. Guess what? These all apply to you too. How is that for stirring up your faith in the love of God? If you are ever in doubt of His love, I encourage you to repeat the sentences above to yourself to remind yourself. Say them out loud and with conviction as often as necessary. Don't allow anyone or anything to move you or change your mind.

God is still telling me, each and every day, to get out of myself and to get up because there are lambs and sheep that still need to be fed. One of the things He constantly brings back to my remembrance is a revelation He gave me quite some time ago, and I will share it with you. It's very simple but quite true. He said, "Just as your life depended upon Jesus' obedience (giving His life on the cross as a ransom for yours), someone else's life is dependent upon your obedience (doing what I have commanded you to do)."

How is that for a thought provoking revelation?

This revelation helped me to see that in the big scheme of things, it's not about me, and just like you, I have a commission to carry out in the earth. I am going to feed His lambs. I am going to feed His sheep because sheep beget sheep. How about you?

"Put out into the deep [water], and lower your nets for a haul." Luke 5:4

In this biblical story, Jesus is standing by the Sea of Galilee teaching, and He is watching while the fishermen bring in their boats and begin to wash their nets. He got into one of the boats that belonged to Simon (Peter) and requested him to pull away a little from the shore. Then Jesus continued to teach the people from the boat.

When He had finished teaching, Jesus told Simon to put out into the deep water and lower his nets for a haul. Simon explained to Jesus that he, along with the other fishermen, had worked all night and hadn't caught a thing, but because Jesus had told them to, they would lower their nets again. Simon had a "nevertheless" moment. He heard the Word. He acted on the Word. He believed the Word even though they had fished all night with nothing to show for their efforts.

Jesus rewarded him for the use of his boat and for having obeyed Him. The Bible says that once they lowered their nets, they caught so many fish that the nets were stretched to the point of breaking. Simon and the other fishermen had to call for help because the haul of fish had been so great.

Life Lesson

At the time the Lord began using this scripture to minister to me, I had been working for the same company for a number of years. I pretty much knew the workplace inside and out. I was sure of my footing and of my place within the company. In other words, my tenure there provided high levels of security and familiarity for me.

As the Lord began to minister the scripture to me, He explained that I was standing in shallow waters within that company. Shallow waters? What did that mean? The water level was low enough that I could see my feet at all times, which meant I could control the water's ability to overtake me. My position and tenure assured my secure footing, and because of it, I didn't allow myself to be completely dependent upon God. I didn't need complete dependence on Him, or so I thought. After all, I could see my feet in the water. I had things under control. In retrospect, I realize that I wanted to be in the driver's seat of my life full-time, and I liked it. Who is in the driver's seat of your life?

My trust and dependence was in me, myself, and I and the time that I had invested in the company, but God was telling me it was time to launch out into the deep and get ready for a haul. "Lord, you want me to launch out where, and get ready for a what?" I wasn't entirely sure what He meant. I sensed that a major change was in the air. If that was the case, I wanted to know what it was going to be in advance so that I could decide whether or not I would like it and accept it. Presumptuous? I am just being honest.

I began to take the scripture apart looking for clues that would provide me with some meaning relative to what God wanted me to do. My attention was drawn to the "deep" part of that command. I knew in my spirit the imminent change involved uncharted waters, and the waters were going to be over my head. Was I going to have to go somewhere? I wasn't sure I was going to like deep waters because I was used to shallow waters. I had control in them.

A haul? What kind of a haul did the Lord have in mind? It just didn't make sense to my carnal mind to leave the security of my surroundings, the sure footing, to potentially go to a place about which I was unsure, and once I got there, what was I going to haul or acquire?

You have to understand how I am "wired." I like the blueprint upfront so that I can weigh all the factors to determine the best possible outcome for me. Does this sound like anyone you might know? I am not real good with the "go with the flow" mentality. It's challenging for me; and sometimes, it causes me to "stay in the huddle" too long thinking and rethinking.

Along with the uncertainty that was presenting itself to me, through the scripture, I also felt fear about the impending change or changes that I anticipated were inevitably going to come into my life. Change is such a small word, but it can have such a major affect. If you're anything like me, you don't always welcome it with open arms and tell it to pull up a chair and stay a minute.

God was telling me to come out of the shallowness of the familiar and come into a deeper place (in Him) where the waters were over my head. I don't want to get ahead of my testimony, but I want to pause here long enough to tell you that although the "deeper place" involved a geographical move, it also involved coming into a deeper relationship with the Lord. It involved a heart change. There was some depth to my relationship with Him, but for where He was going to take me, and is still taking me, my roots had to go deeper. They had to be more securely rooted and grounded in Him.

    I don't know about you, but I am not particularly fond of deep waters. Deeper waters meant that I wouldn't be able to be sure of my footing. I would have to depend upon Him to lead and guide me in this new and unfamiliar place. The idea of "letting go" and "letting God" into the driver's seat of my life was scary. How is that for transparency? It's liberating!

From day one, I had always been "in control" of my life, or so I thought. Sound familiar? God was asking me, because He is a gentleman, to untie my boat from the dock and allow Him to take it where He wanted it to go without an advance itinerary. All of this was being done for my benefit; although, I did not realize it fully at the time. All I could see was change.

In retrospect, I realized that my boat was my life, my will. God was asking me to allow Him to be in complete control of both of them. Not only would His request require me to place myself entirely in His capable and trustworthy Hands, but I would also have to renew my mind to a concept that held very faint familiarity for me: divine direction.

For a very long time, I didn't know that there was such a thing as divine direction, let alone living my life by it. I thought that once you arrived on the planet, you directed your own life. I have since discovered that as my Creator, God has provided me with a set of instructions, the Bible, which should govern my life as His creation. He's the manufacturer, and I am the product. In order for my life to run effectively and fruitfully, the way God intended, the manufacturer's instructions must be carried out properly.

Oftentimes, when a boat is set afloat, it might drift for a while, or be carried away by some rough waters, or be caught in a storm, or it might even end up shipwrecked at the wrong destination. What I had not realized was that if God was calling me out into the deep, He would be with me. The Bible says deep calls unto deep (Psalm 42:7). He was not going to leave me or forsake me (Hebrews 13:5). At the appointed time, He would anchor my boat at its predestined destination to remain there until He instructed otherwise.

My lightning fast mind, on the other hand, reminded me there were many unknowns embedded in what God was asking me to do. It wasn't too sure that I should comply with His request. "If you are going to untie your boat from the dock, shouldn't you at least have a map and a compass to guide you? At least they could give you some kind of indication where you might be headed so that you can make a decision based on that information," said my mind.

My mind had to think about and understand the details before I could make a move, which at times causes me to be "stuck." These kinds of considerations, when coupled with hesitation, can be paralyzing. They will keep you from moving forward according to God's divine direction. I am not saying that you should just jump into something on a whim, but what I am saying is that we have to learn to trust God, even when we don't have all the answers and/or understanding initially. He will guide us every step of the way, if we will just take that first step and believe Him. Sometimes, you just have to turn your head off and check with the umpire of peace (Colossians 3:15). If there is peace in your spirit about a thing, go ahead and pull up your anchor and get out there. God will give you instructions "as you go." I think this last phrase is important enough to say again. He'll be your map and your compass "as you go;" and in the process, you will not only stir up your faith but execute the faith that is pleasing and satisfactory to Him (Hebrews 11:6).

I am reminded of another illustration, relative to allowing God to be in the driver's seat of my life that He showed me while driving to church one morning. It was very dark on the road on which I was traveling, and I couldn't use my high beams to see any farther down the road because there were other cars coming towards me. At best, I could only see a few yards in front of me. God said, "Do you see how you can only see so far in front of you? That's how I want to lead your life." I understood immediately what He meant, and I was grateful that He used my particular learning style to help me to understand. He knows I am a visual learner, so He used a visual example to teach me a lesson. How cool is that?

Uncertainty and fear about "the deep" gave way to my asking God if He realized my life had always been driven with me in the driver's seat. I don't know if the

Holy Spirit had ever been in my driver's seat, and if He had been, the time was of short duration. Of course God knew who had been in the driver's seat of my life. He was giving me this opportunity to mature in Him by letting go of the familiar and allowing Him to show me great and mighty things that I did not know. It was time to change drivers. By the way, maturation in God is an ongoing process, and He gives us daily opportunities to mature in Him that we don't want to miss. Take advantage of them.

    I was then, and I still am, one of those people who likes to have all the pros and cons of a situation laid out before me to review before I am willing to step out or make a decision. I am not much of a risk-taker.

Are you? I have since learned though, with God, sometimes you have to "step out" to "find out," and if it's not God, He will redirect your steps to get you back on the correct path. It took me a while, but I finally discovered that it's okay to admit that I missed God. It's okay for you and I to make a mistake. That's how we learn what is of God and what is not of God. In the aftermath, these kinds of experiences with Him can be used to guide future decision making. He may not always do things the same way, but He always does them in line with His Word. He will never depart from it, no matter what. Of this, we can rest assured.

Unsure steps require faith, but we walk by faith, and not by sight (2 Corinthians 5:7). It's just that simple. OK, but what about the plan that I have devised to help me take these new steps? "A man's mind plans his way, but the Lord directs his steps and makes them sure" (Proverbs 16:9). How clear is that? I have to pause here and praise God for having an answer for every situation and/or circumstance that we, His children, experience. He already provided them even before the foundation of the world, which translates into the time before you and I were ever born. You are awesome, Father! Thank You!

Meanwhile back at the ranch, or should I say dock? I was saying, "Lord, don't you know that all of this is new to me, and that I am very much concerned about letting go and following what I sense is Your direction?" Of course He did, and that's why He was trying to develop, in me, a greater, deeper understanding of who He is so I could learn to lean my "entire personality on Him in Christ in absolute trust and confidence in His power, His wisdom, and His goodness" (Hebrews 6:12). I haven't "arrived" in this area, but each day, several times a day, I meditate on the scripture that states, "I trust in the Lord with all of my heart, and I lean not unto my own understanding. In all of my ways, I acknowledge Him, and He directs my path" (Proverbs 3:5-6). Sometimes, I will even say, "Lord, I don't understand, but I trust

You." As I do this, my faith increases, and my soul (my mind, my will, and my emotions) is able to rest. I <u>choose</u> to believe my steps are ordered by the Lord (Psalm 37:23), and I will always be in the right place at the right time, <u>if</u> I allow Him to lead me.

I pray often that my Father will continue to help me become more comfortable with not always knowing. Simply put, I don't always have to know, but I know and trust in the One who knows. He will never fail me or lie to me. My confidence is in Him. The Bible tells me to cast not away my confidence because it has a great recompense of reward (Hebrews 10:35). You just can't go wrong when your confidence and trust are in Him.

Remember that I mentioned that I was anticipating some impending changes in my life? Hold on to your sailor's cap. The background to this "deep" and "haul" business, is that God had put it on my heart for me and my family to move to another state to join a particular church. He told me,

> Get out of your country, from your family and from your father's house to a land that I will show you. I will make you a great nation; I will bless you and make your name great, and you shall be a blessing. I will bless those who bless you, and I will curse those who curse you; and in you all of the families of the earth will be blessed. (Genesis 12:1-3)

I have to be honest with you and tell you that because I was so focused on relocating, I completely overlooked all the wonderful promises contained within these scriptures. They were certainly possibilities in my life; however, they could only come to pass if I believed and obeyed all I had heard from the Lord. All I could see was that He wanted my boat to travel a great distance to a place, 800 miles to be exact, that was unknown to me and to my family. The only shred of familiarity associated with the move was that I did know a little bit about the "particular" church to which God was calling me. I had been a partner with its ministry for a number of years.

In fact, I had had a chance to visit the ministry during a partner's convention. This is when the Lord spoke to me about moving and joining this church. When I heard Him, I immediately filtered the idea through my mental rolodex looking for some semblance of rationalization. I was unable to find a match, so I tossed the idea to the back of my mind and left it there for several days. During the Sunday service, for which I remained an extra day while visiting, the Lord ministered to me once again that I was to relocate and join this particular church. I heard it as clearly as a bell, but I didn't move. I watched, after the service, as potential members were being shown to an upper room where they would be taken through the membership process knowing that I should have been accompanying them.

When the Spirit of the Lord is upon me, the bottoms of my feet become extremely tingly. It's that feeling you get when your foot has fallen asleep. You know? Well, when He wants me to move or to kneel, the sensation begins to move up my leg. As I stood there watching the people leave the room, the sensation became more intense as it began to move up my legs. I heard the Lord say, "Yvonne, if you don't do it now (join the church), you may never get another chance." Did you know that God is not obligated to present something to us more than once? I almost missed my chance because of my mental reasoning.

With my mind struggling for a hint of rationalization in what I had heard and in what I was about to do, I ran off towards the room where they had taken the others to declare my membership. Once

I submitted my information and was leaving the new members area, I began to think about how I was going to tell my husband what I had done as a result of what I had heard. This task would be nothing short of extremely difficult because he did not know Jesus Christ as his Lord and Savior at the time. How do you begin to explain to an unsaved loved one that the Lord has spoken to you, and He is requiring you to leave behind everything and everyone you have ever known and move to a place that is essentially unknown to you? Only God knows.

My husband had not accompanied me on this trip, but he did know that I enjoyed the visit immensely through our conversations over the telephone. In fact,

I remember wishing and orally expressing to him my desire to remain and eventually move there, just because I liked it. God knows how to give us the desires of our hearts even before we are aware of the desire. He is very methodical in His efforts. He "set me up" when it came to my opportunity to make the trip to visit the church that I would eventually join.

One of the members of the church's ministry, who knew me in a roundabout way through my daughter, sent a pair of airline tickets for her and I to visit at the time the partner's convention was taking place at the church. Was that God or what? You better believe it was! Needless to say, I had a lovely time visiting with the other ministry partners while getting an "up close" look at both the church and the ministry. You must understand that my knowledge and understanding of the ministry was limited to what I had seen on the television broadcast, but I had always had a desire to visit when the partner's convention was taking place each year. How much can you glean from a thirty minute television broadcast?

Over time, I discovered that we don't choose our church, God does. I had never heard that before. I always thought that my church was to be one of my own choosing based on whether or not I liked certain aspects of it. This is not the case from God's perspective. He knows exactly where our particular gifts, talents, and abilities are needed along with knowing where we are to obtain our food for spiritual growth and maturity. He told Elijah to go to a "certain brook" and "there" He would feed him (1 Kings 17:2-4). Had Elijah not done what God told him to do, he would have missed the opportunity that God had arranged for him to be fed. Not only would he have starved due to a famine in the land, but he would have been disobedient to God in the process. When you and I are in covenant with the church and/or ministry that God has chosen for us, He assigns us a shepherd who will watch over our souls. A spiritual covering is particularly important in that the shepherd will often intercept warfare sent to slaughter the sheep. He is also the one who will keep us up in prayer.

Life Lessons for Renewing the Mind - Volume I

I am getting a little ahead of myself, but I want to take a slight detour here and say that I experienced rapid and tremendous spiritual growth at my place called "there." I know without a shadow of a doubt that the church God sent me to was the right one for that season and time in my life. In addition, I understood that I was to bring my gifts, talents, and abilities to the table to assist my spiritual leaders in fulfilling the vision that God had given them. My reward or haul (remember?) from God for my obedience has been wholeness in every area of my life. The wonderful thing is that He's not finished. That was just the beginning. Praise Him!

Back to my story………………… I was now faced with not only sharing with my husband what I had heard and done, but I needed him to agree with me about the move. First Corinthians 2:14 states:

> . . . . the natural, non-spiritual man does not accept or welcome or admit into his heart the gifts and teachings and revelations of the Spirit of God, for they are folly (meaningless nonsense) to him; and he is incapable of knowing them [of progressively recognizing, understanding, and becoming better acquainted with them] because they are spiritually discerned and estimated and appreciated.

Additionally, he and I would have to come into agreement about the move because it was going to impact all of our lives, not just mine. Amos 3:2 asks, "Can two walk together unless they are agreed?" God's desire for the marriage covenant is that the two covenant partners walk together in agreement; otherwise, there will be discord and strife.

I knew my husband would have a difficult time accepting and understanding what God had told me. Needless to say, we argued about it endlessly, and I finally told him that I would move with or without him, but I was going to obey God and make the move. Please understand that I am not advocating any type of rebellion in the marriage covenant.

In reality, saved or unsaved, this man was still my husband, and it was not the will of God that I should leave him to make this move even though I wanted to obey God. Finally, I had no choice but to turn the situation over to the Lord by stating that if He wanted us to make the move, He would have to make it happen. Duh! God knew in advance about the difficulty we were going to have in coming to an agreement about it. While I was trying to figure it out, He had already worked the situation out according to His plan. He was just waiting for me to give up trying to "make it happen" in my strength and step aside so He could make it happen in His (more of the deep stuff). His strength and power are made strong and show themselves most effectively in our weaknesses (2 Corinthians 22:9). This move was His will for us, and He had already made a way for it to happen. Of course, I only came to that realization in hindsight. It takes a minute for me to catch on sometimes, remember?

I completely understood my husband's perspective and reluctance. In the natural, this move would require us to launch our boat into uncharted waters that would take us quite a distance away from the city of our births, family, friends, jobs, etc. To my natural mind, it just didn't make sense to leave these things to venture to an unfamiliar place, so I know it didn't make sense to him.

Have you ever experienced conflict between your spirit and your flesh? My spirit was saying, "Yes," but the mind of my flesh was saying, "No! Hello? It doesn't make sense." Additionally, I had plenty of discouragement from people (the naysayers) all along the way which only added to the anxiety, uncertainty, and fear that I was feeling about the move. In hindsight, I have come to realize that they were decoys that had been sent to distract me. They had been sent to cause me to take my eyes off of what the Lord had told me to do and to focus on all the reasons why the move just didn't make any sense to my flesh. My spirit, however, was at rest. My umpire said there was peace there. Relative to my husband's spirit, his was dead to God because Jesus did not live in him, so spiritually speaking he had no understanding. He was only able to understand with his mind, and his mind was telling him the same thing my mind was telling me: "It doesn't make sense." Spiritual things appear as foolishness to the mind. It's a square peg round hole combination, and there is, without a doubt, no fit.

God was trying to direct my life, as well as my husband's even though he didn't know it (yet). Have you ever felt Him trying to direct yours? People will sometimes remark that "something told them" something in a situation. That something is the third person of the Trinity: the Holy Spirit. I have discovered that by allowing God in the driver's seat of my life, I have been led onto the profitable paths of life. God always has my best interest at heart. Even when I make a wrong move or fall short of His instruction, He is faithful and caring enough to get me back on the right path. Thank you, Jesus!

Did you know that as believers, you and I have a blood-bought right to have direction from our Father? In my daily prayer time, I confess that confusion is not a part of my life. I have the wisdom of God because I ask for it. I know the voice of my Good Shepherd, and the voice of a stranger I just flat out refuse to follow (John 10:4-5). How do I know it is God speaking? God always speaks in line with His word. That's why it is so vital to meditate on the Word of God day and night (Joshua 1:8), so that when you are given a direction, you can line that direction up with God's Word and discern whether or not it is God speaking. Without knowing the Word, you are taking a risk that could come back to haunt you in the long run.

Well, the move didn't take place right away. As a matter of fact, it was two years in the making for a variety of reasons. Apart from my husband's reluctance, which rested primarily on his years of service on his job and his lack of spiritual understanding, one of the major reasons the move was delayed was the fact that we were building a house. How is that for adding drama to the story? The foundation had already been laid, and the materials had been assembled to start building. We were particularly excited about this house because it was the first time for both me and my husband that we had had a chance to build a house from the ground up with our particular specifications.

What I didn't tell you is that I knew in my spirit that I should have consulted God initially to see if building a house, <u>at that time</u>, was His will for us. Sometimes, a thing can be in the will of God for you and me, but it must have the right timing: God's timing. On several occasions, I have found out the hard way that timing is essential in the things of God. In retrospect, I recall that a feeling of uncertainty, you know that little nagging feeling in the back of your mind or the pit of your stomach, was constantly with me relative to buying a house at that time. I forged ahead anyway ignoring the feeling and hoping that God would bless what we had started in the flesh. Keep in mind that I knew I had heard from the Lord relative to the move, but I was trying in my little finite mind to find a way to have my house and to make the move that He was requiring of us so that I would not be disobeying Him. In other words, I wanted to delay my obedience so that I could "have my cake and eat it too." It seemed like a good idea at the time, but God would never have been pleased with it, and things would not have worked out the way that I would have desired in the long run.

    I wanted to make a deal with God about that new house. Imagine that! I must have been out of my mind. Have you ever tried to make a deal with the Lord? He doesn't play "Let's Make a Deal." Very simply, it's His way because it's the best way. I reasoned that if He allowed me to live in that new house for about two years time, I would make the move afterwards. That was <u>not</u> God's plan for us. I struggled the whole time with trying to make a distinction between whether what I was feeling was simply nerves about the whole process of building a new house or about being out of the will of God for my life. I have to tell you that I didn't need to check with my umpire of peace because I didn't want to hear what His answer was going to be. There was no uncertainty about what we were to do in this situation. Obey God, and relocate. Enough said. I was trying to be wise in my own eyes, but what I was really being was a fool. The Bible reiterates my point in 1 Corinthians 3:18-20 by stating:

> Stop deceiving yourselves. If you think you are wise by this world's standards, you need to become a fool to be truly wise. For the wisdom of this world is foolishness to God. As the Scriptures say, He traps the wise in the snare of their own cleverness. And again, the Lord knows the thoughts of the wise; he knows they are worthless.

Down deep, I knew that building a house was not the will of God for our lives, at that time, because He wouldn't have required the move had His will been otherwise. The Bible says that the blessings of the Lord will make you rich, and He adds no sorrow with it (Proverbs 10:22). I can tell you that I was experiencing sorrow about that house, and it hadn't even been built yet.

In the end, we didn't get the house because it was simply not God's plan for us then. As I said, I didn't have a peace about it, but what I did have was a strong peace about the relocation even though my mind couldn't create a rationale for it. Once again, in retrospect, I had never given any thought to what I might have missed if I had delayed the move by the "if you let me live in the new house for two years deal" that I was trying to make with God. He saw the big picture, and He knew "why" we had to make the move "when" we were to make it. It was not for me to know at that time, but I believe there would have been many missed opportunities, for me personally, to mature spiritually had we not moved when God said.

He knew there were people who were waiting for what He could sow into their lives through my gifts, talents, and abilities. The idea that I was being selfish never even crossed my mind, but that's what it was: selfishness. I hadn't given a moment's thought to someone else possibly needing what I could bring to the table because my focus was on me and what I wanted at the time. I mistakenly thought that it was all about me. God didn't agree with my idea of being "self-absorbed." Jesus told His disciples that He came into the earth to serve not to be served and to give His life as a ransom for many (Mark 10:45).

We must understand that God's overall plan in the earth will never be distressed or foiled because you or I fail to hear and to obey His instructions. It will be carried out, but He would like to use you and me in the process. What an awesome and fulfilling privilege it is to know you have been instrumental in helping to improve someone else's life. The Bible says some of us will plant, others will water, but God will bring forth the increase in them at the appointed time (1 Corinthians 3:6). The key is you and I have to be willing to be a planter and/or a waterer at a moment's notice. We have to be ever ready for every good work (Titus 3:1). Amen!

Life Lessons for Renewing the Mind - Volume I

God has a way of getting our attention, and He got mine as I continued to forge ahead with the house building project. Besides the uncertainty surrounding the house, we were suddenly faced with unemployment. As I stated earlier, I had turned my husband over to God because I couldn't change his mind about moving. I had grown weary of the endless battles of trying to convince him this was something we had to do. This man came home two days after the 9/11 incident and told me he had been laid off permanently, from his place of employment, after twenty-five plus years. Needless to say, I was devastated. I felt like someone had just sucker punched me in the stomach. My thoughts immediately raced to the house. I remember the Spirit of the Lord reminding me that I could have what I said, so before I said anything in response to the unemployment news, I had to grab hold of my mind because it was racing. I got on the phone with a longtime friend of mine and asked her to encourage me in the Lord. She helped me to redirect my thoughts to the Word of God. Once my thoughts were going in the right direction, my mouth was able to get on board and speak the Word so life could be brought into the situation.

Trials, tests, and troubles are a part of life, but they do <u>not</u> change the Word of God. It still accomplishes what it has been sent out to do. God does not fail, He does not lie, and His Word is true. Hallelujah!

What were we going to do now that we were being forced to deal with the unemployment issue? The house was certainly no longer a possibility with the reduction in income. To make matters worse, we had several thousand dollars invested, up front, in our particular architectural modifications for the house. Would we be able to recover any of that money, or would we just have to take a loss? Although it required quite a bit of time, praise God, we did recover a substantial portion of that investment.

With the loss of both the house and the job, I guess the idea of moving sort of settled in over the two of us. We certainly had nothing to lose by at least entertaining the idea. For me, the possibility of making deals with God was now null and void. As for my husband, he could no longer use the time invested in his job as an excuse for not moving; although in the final outcome, his years of service worked in his favor. A few months later, while perusing the internet in search of a job in the city to which we were inevitably going to move, my husband found a job opening in our new city with the same company from which he had just received the permanent layoff. He submitted a resume, went for a job interview, got the job, and moved into our new home a few months later.

Coincidence? I think not. Luck? There's no such thing

in God. That was all the Lord's doing, and it was a marvelous thing in our eyes even to this day (Psalm 118:23)!

Although everything was new and uncharted for us in our new city and state, God was faithful. He provided everything we needed, and more, to get settled in where He docked our boat. One of the key things that I learned through this experience is to not become too tied to one particular place or thing to the point where you cannot make any changes. Let me help you. There may come a time when God will require you and I to come out into yet another deeper level, in Him, in some area of life, which could include a major change of some kind. If that should happen, rest assured. God will be faithful to whatever He has called us to do. Our part is to obey Him and follow Him wherever He chooses to lead. He is the Shepherd and we are the sheep. Psalm 23 expresses the shepherd and sheep relationship beautifully. It says:

> The Lord is my shepherd; I shall not want. He makes me lie down in green pastures; He leads me beside the still waters. He restores my soul. He leads me in the paths of righteousness for His name's sake. Yea, though I walk through the valley of the shadow of death, I will fear no evil; for You are with me. Your rod and your staff, they comfort me. You prepare a table before me in the presence of my enemies; You anoint my head with oil; my cup runs over. Surely goodness and mercy shall follow me all the days of my life; And I will dwell in the house of the Lord, forever.

God always has higher heights and deeper depths into which He wants to take us. I am a witness. In the years since we moved to our new home and church, I have experienced both higher heights and deeper depths repeatedly. It has never been easy, but I don't believe I have ever been as spiritually mature and as stable in the Lord as I am today. Again, I have not "arrived," but I know I couldn't have come this far had I not obeyed the Lord. I would have missed a date with divine destiny had I chosen to disobey Him and remain in the shallow waters of familiarity.

    I visit my hometown a couple of times each year, and I can now see some things there that I could not see before. I stand sometimes on one of the main streets hoping to meet with old acquaintances along with the opportunity to observe any changes in the city. I feel like the ostrich who has finally had its head pulled out from the sand in that I "see" now. Before the move, my head was buried in darkness like so many others, but now Jesus has opened the eyes of my understanding to the deeper things in Him. I don't mean to imply that I am better than anyone else there, but rather I have become a new creature in Christ, and the old things have passed away. All things have become new (2 Corinthians 5:17). With this newness, I have learned to have a new compassion and love for others, that I did not have before, especially when I can see that some of them are still in the darkness of not knowing Jesus Christ as Lord and Savior. I don't mind telling you that the compassion and love for others, of which I spoke, has matured in me.

This level of love and compassion for others gives me an opportunity to invite God into someone's situation by learning to pray the Word of God over it. Prayer is one of the most powerful ways to cause an individual to cultivate and mature in the love of God. If you are struggling with something about someone, pray for them, and watch how quickly God will either change your heart, or the other person's heart, or both. He responds to prayer.

Romans 2:4 says, "It's the goodness of God that will draw all men to repentance." Knowing this, I try to be good to people in His strength, not my own. I share the Word with them wherever and whenever the opportunity presents itself. This is the essence of salvation. God doesn't just save us for ourselves, but He saves us for others as well.

As you and I continue to attend a Bible-based church where we can be fed and equipped, the Lord expects us to continue to do the work of the ministry by sharing the good news with others until the imminent return of Jesus Christ.

Be mindful that Jesus is soon to come. Be a discerner of the time, so you will not get caught unaware when He arrives. If you are caught at all, then be caught being an ambassador for Christ (2 Corinthians 5:20) who refuses to bring a reproach upon the name of the Lord. Be one of those who will meditate on the Word God both day and night, so that you will be able to speak a Word in season to him that is weary (Isaiah 50:4).

"For God is not unjust to forget your work and labor of love which you have shown toward His name, in that you have ministered to the saints and do minister."
Hebrews 6:10

Let me begin by stating that you and I don't have to belong to a church or a have a pulpit to be able to minister to others. One definition of the word "minister" means to give aid or service. Another defines the term as acting or active as an agent; instrumental. It took a minute for me to understand this word in a broader context. My definition of the word minister was limited to the cleric and/or officiate of a particular church who "ministered" or preached encouraging words to hurting people from the pulpit. S/he was the person who wore the white collar around the neck sometimes and sat on the front pews with all the other dignitaries. S/he had a title before his or her name. Let me clarify my statements by saying that I am not minister bashing. I simply want you to understand my concept of the word.

Over the course of time, my understanding of "who" a minister is and just what it means to "minister" was enlightened as well as broadened. First, I discovered that Jesus didn't save me just for me. By the same token, He didn't save you just for you. Were you aware of that? He saved each of us to assist in building up the Kingdom of God. Second, because of our membership in the Body of Christ, we have been called to be ambassadors or representatives in the earth for Him who has called us out of darkness and into the marvelous light. Read over the next few scriptures slowly, and you will see what I mean.

> But all things are from God, Who through Jesus Christ reconciled us to Himself [received us into favor, brought us into harmony with Himself] and gave to us the ministry of reconciliation [that by word and deed we might aim to bring others into harmony with Him]. It was God [personally present] in Christ, reconciling and restoring the world to favor with Himself, not counting up and holding against [men] their trespasses [but canceling them], and committing to us the message of reconciliation (of the restoration to favor). So we are Christ's ambassadors, God making His appeal as it were through us. We [as Christ's personal representatives] beg you for His sake to lay hold of the divine favor

[now offered you] and be reconciled to God. (2 Corinthians 5:18-20)

An ambassador is one who is an authorized representative or messenger. Every believer has been called to be an ambassador for Christ. In other words, because I have accepted Jesus Christ as my Lord and as my Savior, I have become His messenger or representative in the earth, which involves ministering to people. The word "people" covers a wide range of individuals including those who are not like you and me, the unlovely, those who would spitefully use us, those outside of our personal circle of churchgoing buddies, our friends and acquaintances, etc.

Jesus is coming back for a church, His Body, without spot, blemish, or wrinkle (Ephesians 5:27). That means that we should be ever pressing towards becoming more like Him on the inside so we can assist others with whom we come into contact. The Bible says we should consecrate (set aside for a purpose) ourselves to God while engaging in holy behaviors and developing Christlike qualities (2 Peter 3:11). We have to learn how to let go of the world and allow God to do a work in us and through us so we can become an asset to the Body of Christ. The book of 2 Timothy 2:21 emphasizes this point equally as well:

> So whoever cleanses himself [from what is ignoble and unclean, who separates himself from contact with contaminating and

corrupting influences] will [then himself] be a vessel set apart and useful for honorable and noble purposes, consecrated and profitable to the Master, fit and ready for any good work.

I believe God gives you and me ample time and opportunity to make the necessary changes. The Bible describes the Lord as long-suffering because He desires that none should perish, but that all should come to repentance (2 Peter 3:9). Thank God that you and I can get the process of ministering to others started by simply accepting Jesus Christ as our Lord and Savior. It's that simple.

In the meantime, you and I may be the only Jesus with whom an unbeliever and sometimes even a believer comes into contact or even sees, and we have to be ready to minister. Simply put, we have to be ready to boldly and unashamedly share with others, in words and in deeds, the good news of the gospel of Jesus Christ. We have to be ready to testify to people about who God is and what He has done in our lives. We overcome by the blood of the Lamb and the "word" of our testimony (Revelation 12:11).

Beyond the words and the deeds, we have to know, for ourselves, what the Word of God has to say about how to live our everyday lives. It's very difficult to encourage, to exhort, to comfort, and to build others up in the Word of God if you don't know what it says, and it hasn't become real in your life.

Time spent meditating in the Word will yield wonderful personal benefits, but I can honestly say the greater rewards come when you know and can see that you have been able to have an impact on someone else's life for Christ. Ministering for the Lord will require you to love people, even when they don't love you. While love and ministering go together like a hand in glove, you may recall that the scripture that appears at the beginning of this text describes our commission to minister as a "labor of love." Labor is equated with work. A "labor of love" involves work that may not always be easy and/or feel good to the flesh. The scripture says it is work that is carried out in the name of the Lord. Jesus has given us two commandments:

> And He replied to him, You shall love the Lord your God with all your heart and with all your soul and with all your mind (intellect). This is the great (most important, principal) and first commandment. And a second is like it: You shall love your neighbor as (you do) yourself. These two commandments sum up and upon them depend all the Law and the Prophets. (Matthew 22:37-40)

Let me assure you that there is a reward attached to loving others that can come only from God who does not forget what you and I have done in and for His name's sake.

I use to have such a limited understanding of the word love when it came to people outside of my immediate sphere. I thought I only had to love my relatives and outside of them, only those I chose to love. From God's perspective, this is simply not the case. It's shortsightedness and selfishness. I was following the first commandment about loving the Lord, but I placed a limitation on the second one. It was quite some time before I realized that if I was saying that I really "loved the Lord," I would keep <u>all</u> of His commandments (John 14:15). All the commandments are based upon the two I have already mentioned: Loving the Lord your God and loving your neighbor as you love yourself.

The book of 1 John 4 gives us a clear understanding of love. I encourage you to spend some time meditating in it. It's all good. It states that God is love (4:8), and that we love Him because He first loved us (4:19). Furthermore, because He loved us, we ought to love one another (4:11). Would you agree that verse 11 is easier said than done?

Let me take it one step further and refresh both of our memories to the fact that those "others" include our enemies, the unlovely, the unsaved, the saved, those who would spitefully use us, those who get on our last nerve, etc. Knowing this, we are then faced with the following scripture in 1 John 4:20:

> If anyone says, I love God, and hates (detests, abominates) his brother [in Christ], he is a liar; for he who does not love his brother, whom he has seen, cannot love God, whom he has not seen.

Now, we become responsible for what we've heard, and God will certainly remind us of it. We will also be tested in this area. I can guarantee it because testing is one of the ways spiritual fruit is developed. At various times, I have failed the test, but because He loves me, the Lord continues to give me an opportunity to raise the productivity level in my love walk. And because I love Him, I now have to learn how to love my brothers and sisters whether I want to or not. I don't try to do it my strength, or ability, or wisdom because when I do, I fail. I rely on the Comforter: The Holy Spirit to help me.

May I emphasize again that learning how to love people is no easy task. Rest assured. God will always allow people into our circle who are not like us on purpose because everyone "needs" to love and to be loved. One of the greatest gifts you or I can give another person is the gift of love. In fact, the Bible calls love the greatest gift among the three gifts of faith, hope, and love (1 Corinthians 13).

Time for the test……………………………… that would help me to develop the fruit called love.

Life Lesson

Has the Lord ever led you to become part of a particular group of people so that you could bring your gifts, talents, and abilities to the table? Have you ever heard the term "spiritual employment?" I had never heard the term before joining my new church, nor had I given much thought to bringing my assets to a particular subgroup of a ministry of a church with the goal of doing my part in contributing to the fulfillment of the church's vision. I don't mean to imply that my reasons for joining any group were selfish ones, but rather the idea of "serving" in a subgroup connected to a church was rather foreign to me. I had never had this kind of experience or mindset while I was a member of any church. As a matter of fact, for quite some time, I was just one of those folks who "attended" church. Nothing more. Nothing less. I was just an attendee "taking up space" and "sucking up air" each week that the doors opened.

So, I had been introduced to the term "spiritual employment," and I had to decide exactly what that would be for me. Because I had always sung in some sort of group since my early teens, and music had always been near and dear to my heart, I decided to audition for the choir. It was a very "natural selection" for me given my love for music.

I participated in the audition process, like everyone else, and within a short period of time, I found myself a new member of my church's choir. I remember the day I received the news that I was being accepted into the group. I was so excited, but little did I know that the Lord had so much more in store for me as well as for the choir.

I will also say that He, being God all by Himself, could see the end from the beginning, and He continued to prepare me all along the way for what was to come. So often in hindsight, I have thanked the Lord for not having told me what was on the road up ahead. I probably would have wanted to sidestep the situation; thereby, robbing myself of an opportunity to experience the goodness of God in my life, not to mention the valuable experience I could gain that would open the door for me to minister to others from a "real" place. There are times, when God will "allow" things to occur in our lives that will cause us to draw closer to Him while spiritually maturing us.

The Word of God says many are the afflictions of the righteous, but the Lord delivers him out of them all (Psalm 34:19). What He didn't tell me was that the afflictions come not only from the unsaved, but they also come from the saved. Yes, that's right. I said they also come from the saints of God. Who would have thought it possible? I will tell you that I had a very difficult time wrapping my head around that notion.

I was so naïve about saved people largely in part because I hadn't had much experience with them. I found out the hard way that although they may look the part, speak the correct Christian jargon, wear a "Jesus" pin, and associate with many of the religious people of the day, they don't always do and/or say the right (godly) thing.

At least with unsaved people you know from where they are coming, and most of the time their actions are overt and obvious. With saved people, ungodly behaviors are more covert and tend to be masked by a fake or phony exterior under which lies the "mind of the flesh" rather than the spirit of a "renewed mind." When the flesh is not being subdued and governed by the spirit, it's out of control. I am telling you what I know from experience, which is why it is so important for the believer to have a renewed mind. It is essential to our spiritual well-being to meditate on the Word of God each day. It give us the "right" focus.

Is it an unreasonable expectation for me to expect saved people to "act" like they're saved? As I use the word "act," I think it may be incorrect in that it suggests phoniness. I expect saved people to be saved "for real," and to be known by their fruits (Matthew 7:16).

"Acting," I believe, is one of the primary reasons why we, the Church, have short-circuited our ability to draw men unto Him. In some cases, we have failed to conduct ourselves any better than the unbeliever. This being the case, why would the unbeliever desire what we have in Christ when there appears to be no noticeable differences between him, the unbeliever, and you and I? In these cases, we run the risk of bringing a reproach to the name of the Lord. That's not good.

The Word of the Lord tells us to test every spirit. We are to try them to see if they proceed from God (1 John 4:1). The Message Bible states it this way:

My dear friends, don't believe everything you hear. Carefully weigh and examine what people tell you. Not everyone who talks about God comes from God. There are a lot of loose preachers in the world.

Yes, this is referring to preachers, or those who are considered spiritual leaders and/or teachers, but I believe that it applies to everyone. I also believe it applies to human behavior in general because each of us lives in a fleshly body that is constantly at war with the spirit.

Once again, I want to emphasize the importance of meditating upon the Word of God so that our minds, and consequently our behaviors, align themselves with it. Relative to others, you can't "try" their spirit and discern whether or not it is of God if you don't "know" God. One of the most direct ways to accomplish this task is to invest time in His Word. Saturate yourself in His Word. God *is* His Word, and if the spirit is of Him, it will line up with the Word. There will be an undeniable, unmistakable match between the two. I assure you.

People are human, and they make mistakes, but is it an inconceivable notion to expect the people with whom you fellowship, hear the same Word on a consistent basis, and even attend the same church to line up their lives with the Word of God to the point where it is manifested in their behaviors? Isn't that how it is supposed to happen? It's called spiritual maturity, isn't it? Am I asking too much of myself and my fellow believers in Christ?

The book of James 1:22 tells us we should not only be "hearers" of the Word but "doers" of the Word. You will notice the scripture does not state we should do only those parts that are pleasing to the flesh. In other words, it doesn't give us the option of doing what we want and leaving the rest to fall by the wayside. God expects us to do all that is written therein (Joshua 1:8).

Allow me to suggest, for some people, things fall into the gray areas of life, and although it may be their reality and a comfort, I, personally, find it characteristic of indecisiveness. For me, things are black and white. Either they are or they aren't, and I make no apologies and/or excuses for my perspective.

This perspective is part of my core belief system, and it's as simple as that for me; in which case, I don't understand it when people appear to be "double-minded." The Bible tells us a double-minded man is unstable in all of his ways. It describes him as hesitating, dubious, irresolute, unreliable and uncertain about everything he thinks, feels, and decides (James 1:8). God has even told us in His Word that He desires that we be hot or cold not lukewarm; otherwise, He will spew us out of His mouth like vomit (Revelation 3:16). I get the feeling that double-mindedness doesn't go over too well with God. How about you?

To further illustrate my point, allow me to bring your attention to the Bible. It is full of dichotomies, or groups of two, where the groups are mutually exclusive or contradictory. For example, God and the devil are contradictory. Other examples include good and evil, light and darkness, righteousness and sin, love and hate, life and death, heaven and hell and so on. I think you get the picture. With this in mind, it would appear that God supports those things that are good and that bring life to our lives. He tells us that He sets before us life and death, and that we should choose life (Deuteronomy 30:19). He didn't say, "Ride the fence where you can get a little of both without committing to one or the other." He says, "Choose life," which indicates that a definite choice has been made.

Why then do we so often choose to go in the opposite direction? I think among a number of possible explanations, the "mind of the flesh" would be a major cause of bad decision making. It must be subdued and crucified each day, if we are to follow Christ and walk in His ways. The Bible says the flesh profits nothing (John 6:63), but by meditating on the Word, we can "make" our way prosperous (Joshua 1:8) and overcome the flesh. As you and I both know, the flesh can be very strong; in which case, we need something even stronger to subdue it: The Word of God and <u>only</u> the Word of God.

At the outset of this particular scenario, I possessed only a superficial understanding of and relatively no experience with some of the concepts I just shared with you in the last few pages. What I did possess was a desire to comply with my pastors' request to become "spiritually employed." My umpire of peace (Colossians 3:15) had given me the "thumbs up" about joining the choir, and as I stated earlier, I was excited about the possibility of bringing my gifts, talents, and abilities to this particular subgroup. This was my reasonable service given the fact that I was "eating" from the ministry's spiritual table each week.

With the audition process behind me, I was "in." I expected to be embraced and welcomed as a new member. This didn't happen for me for what seemed like a very long time. The bottom line to my chagrin was that reality and my expectations, as a new member, did not intersect. What do you do when that happens, and you believe that God has called you to be in that particular place at that particular time? How do you keep from becoming selfish in the flesh by quitting while maintaining a genuine love walk? How do you keep a positive attitude and remember that someone else is waiting on what you have to bring to the table? Although I am getting a little ahead of myself, I wanted to put some questions out there for you to think about before we continue.

Oblivious to what was to come, I gathered up my materials, checked the time, and I was off to my very first rehearsal. I remember entering the room with hope and a smile in earnest expectation of making some new friends and becoming a part "of" as opposed to being a part "from." It didn't take very long before my smile diminished in its brilliance, and my hope, relative to this new undertaking, receded to a back shelf because I was being ostracized or so I thought. Why and for what reason? I began to question whether or not I had made a mistake and chosen the wrong subgroup. I didn't remember signing up for this kind of treatment. Maybe it was just because I was "new," but wouldn't that have been all the more reason to make me feel welcomed?

Over time, my heart became sick (figuratively speaking) as this painful scenario continued to play itself out time and time again during subsequent rehearsals and Sunday morning services. The Bible says that hope deferred makes the heart grow sick, but desire fulfilled is a tree of life (Proverbs 13:12). I can attest to this scripture; however, the fruit of my desire relative to my choir membership and participation would not manifest itself for quite some time. Again, I just wanted to be a part "of" not a part "from," but it appeared that I was being forced to be a part of the latter without my consent and for a while without my knowledge.

I can remember questioning myself over and over again to try to identify something that I was doing that might be causing the problem. Why was this happening to me? I just didn't understand. I was a little slow in catching on to what was obvious. At first, I kept wondering if my imagination was working overtime. Was what I thought was happening "really" happening? Self-assessment and I become good friends. I found out that the only thing of which I was guilty was just being me. For some individuals, that was unacceptable, and I was allowing it to affect me.

The Word says that a man who has friends must show himself friendly (Proverbs 18:24), so in an attempt to counteract what had been happening to me, I attempted to do just that: be a "doer" of the Word. Sadly, my overtures of friendship, were more often than not, rejected by these saved, "church" folk.

Had I missed God? I had to go back and check once again with my umpire of peace, the Holy Spirit, to determine if I was in the right place. The peace of God was certainly present, but if this was how members of the Body of Christ treated each other, then I didn't want any part of it; yet, I couldn't just walk away. My desire to sing was very strong. I know enough about God and how He deals with me to know that when I am supposed to be in a certain place and/or doing a certain thing, He confirms it for me. In this case, the confirmation came through a very subtle, yet gentle pressure upon me from the Hand of God telling me to remain in place. I have since learned that when God is finished with me in a certain area, the pressure will lift like a release.

Remember, I mentioned earlier that God doesn't save us just for ourselves? He saves us with others in mind. In hindsight, I know God allowed the particular challenges associated with my group membership to come my way for my benefit as well as for the benefit of others. In the process of my love walk being tested and tried, the challenges forced me to go to God more often and to meditate in His Word to keep me on the straight and narrow path. I came away with an invaluable testimony that has allowed me to minister to others. Praise God!

One of the most wonderful things I have learned, and I am still learning, about God is that He always has the big picture in mind no matter what the circumstance may be. Oftentimes, we can only see a small portion of it which may cause us some frustration, at least it does for me, and/or lack of understanding. This is where trusting in the Lord to know what's best for us should enter our thinking. It has taken me some time to make progress in the area of casting my cares upon Him. I will forever have to practice it, but I am pleased to know that I am maturing in this area. In fact, I have decided to include the following scripture in my daily prayer time to keep my thoughts and my mouth going in the "right" direction:

> Lean on, trust in, and be confident in the Lord with all your heart and mind and do not rely on your own insight or understanding. In all your ways know, recognize, acknowledge Him, and He will direct and make straight and plain your paths. (Proverbs 3:5-6)

This scripture helps me to get focused on trusting God and believing that He does not fail me or lie to me. He wants nothing but the best for me as His child. I also pray and ask Him to make me comfortable with not always knowing. Have you ever been there? I don't always have to know, but I know the One who knows, and I can rest in that confidence in Him. As a matter of fact, when I feel myself getting anxious, I remind myself that the Lord has been mindful of me (Psalm 115:12); therefore, I can say, "Return to your rest, O my soul, for the Lord has dealt bountifully with you" (Psalm 116:7). In others words, I tell my soul (mind, will, and emotions) to take a seat because God has everything under control.

In spite of my initial experience with the "rejection," I continued to return, time and time again, to satisfy the requirements associated with my choir membership as well as to obey my God. You might wonder if I was being a glutton for punishment. No, that wasn't the plan. I was just determined to remain steadfast and undeterred to my commitment, even with the thorn in my side, until God "released" me. The gentle pressure, that I described earlier from the Hand of God, was still very much present in my life. This was one of those times when He chose to have me "go through" rather than "deliver me from" the unpleasantness and perhaps even the unfairness of the situation. His ways are not our ways. His thoughts are not our thoughts (Isaiah 55:8). He had a purpose in mind, and I had to know that as my Father, He knew what was best for me. I was only able to manage a tunnel vision; whereas, He saw the overall vision and the final outcome. He also knew that the fruit of the Spirit within me required further development.

If you are wondering whether or not the way people treated me continued and/or changed, the answer to both questions is "yes." I experienced the isolation of not only being a newcomer in general, but I was also from a different geographic location that had shaped my outlook on life. Additionally, my personal belief system, my hairstyle, my style of dress, my behaviors, and the straight forward manner in which I dealt with people all seemed to be contrary and offensive to many in this subgroup. People weren't exactly drawn to these things about me. They were more comfortable with the groups or cliques and the status quo that had been established, before my arrival, and they didn't seem to want change nor did they "openly" welcome anyone who might represent any kind of a change.

    I didn't know it then, but I was the mirror God used in various ways to give other people the opportunity to see their true selves while exposing areas that might require them to make some changes. That same mirror also revealed to me some areas in which I needed to change. As I am sure you are aware, change can be very challenging and hard on the flesh. A good scripture to meditate on for change is Psalm 51:10. It says, "Create in me a clean heart, O God, and renew a right, persevering, and steadfast spirit within me."

Needless to say, this was a very lonely time for me, and it went on for quite some time. In some instances, I can remember crying on the way home from church services, in which we sang, because I felt so lonely, unloved and unappreciated. I don't mean to imply that I was there to be noticed, but everyone desires and needs fellowship along with being told from time to time s/he is doing a good job and that s/he is appreciated.

Looking back, I realize this was a time of sowing for me. I had to sow the loneliness, the disappointment, and the offense I was experiencing in order to pursue the will of God for me in this area and to reap a harvest of the fruit of the Spirit. God has promised that we will reap a harvest, if we will continue to do the right thing even when we feel weary (Galatians 6:9). At some point, I had to stop and ask myself why I was there. Was it for Him or for me?

In the midst of all I was feeling and experiencing, I was incapable of realizing that this was an opportunity provided by God that had to be taken while it was available. Do you remember the boat I spoke of in a previous chapter? Well, now that it was docked at my place called "there," God was requiring me to step out of the boat. In other words, He wanted me to step out of my comfort zone. My spiritual maturity and next level in Him were dependent upon my obedience.

    I didn't realize there wouldn't be people in my corner clapping and cheering for me. There were no "welcome wagons" to speak of nor rolling out of the red carpet at my arrival in the choir. There is no vanity being expressed in these statements. I wasn't anyone special. I was just another member of the Body of Christ trying to serve the ministry to which I had been called. No more. No less. I just wanted to be "treated right" as in the loving your neighbor as you love yourself commandment that we are commanded to follow.

Ironically, these were some of the same people I had observed praying for God to send new members; yet, when I arrived, it appeared they had forgotten that they were the ones who had "prayed me in." Had the "right hand of fellowship" become antiquated? Had it become dissociated with new members? I didn't get that email.

Finally, I cried out to God telling Him this kind of treatment was <u>not</u> why I had joined the choir. I felt I was too old to be a part of what I considered immature behaviors and mindsets. I realized immaturity doesn't play favorites. Did I want to quit? You'd better believe I did! The thought crossed my mind on several occasions. Hence, the Lord had to get right in my face with a very direct question: "If you go, how will things ever change?" To tell you the truth, I really didn't care, at that point, whether or not things changed. All I knew was that my emotions were telling me I wanted relief from the situation. My flesh was riding in the driver's seat at this point, and God had to renew my mind and redirect me because it was causing me to lose my focus. I needed my mind renewed "quick and in a hurry" because my flesh was resisting being ousted from the command center of my mind.

Despite my "feelings" (flesh), I made the decision to remain in place. Again, the primary reason was that I knew God had called me to be there, and He had not "released" me. I wanted to be obedient to Him. During those times when I tried to quit and run away, He cared enough about me to hold on to my foot in the spirit and cause me to consider the big picture, as opposed to quitting for selfish reasons. In the aftermath, I appreciated God for His decision to have me remain in place. He also let me know that the time, effort, and energy I had been investing in the choir had not been wasted. Man may not have acknowledged or appreciated me, but He did. He reminded me:

> For God is not unrighteous to forget or overlook your labor and the love which you have shown for His name's sake in ministering to the needs of the saints (His own consecrated people), as you still do.
> (Hebrews 6:10)

I lost sight of the fact that I was there to be of service to the Lord and to His people. The flesh will sometimes rebel in and against service or ministry to others. Needless to say, it was not always easy to serve, but I thank God He redefined my focus and gave me the strength and the grace to remain in my position in the choir.

The Lord helped me to look past the unkind treatment I had received. He required me to relinquish all that had happened to me onto Him and leave it there. He enabled me to begin to reach out to others past my hurt, pain, and disappointment.

In time, my attitude and my outlook began to change relative to the situation. All of a sudden, I didn't want other people to have to experience what I had experienced, so I made every effort to assist in the transition of new members into the choir. I didn't do anything big or spectacular or even worthy of notice. They were simple things like saying "hello" and introducing myself, or lending my music to someone who may not have had it, or bringing along an extra food item to share, or giving someone a smile, or sitting near a new member and striking up a conversation, or making an effort to recall names, etc.

These kinds of efforts made all the difference in the world to <u>me</u> in that they gave me opportunities to mature in God while developing my spiritual fruit. They also taught me how to love people "beyond the words."

I loved my heavenly Father so much that I was willing to do whatever I needed to do to please Him in spite of my feelings and/or the circumstances. He made His position clear. He said love Him, and love others.

Again, I want to reiterate that none of this was easy. It was very hard on my flesh, but God did not forget what He had asked me to do in putting aside my discontentment and loneliness in lieu of carrying out His will as a "labor of love." I did what I did to the glory of His name. Even though what He was asking me to do may not always have manifested itself in words, I believe that it ministered to His people, and as I ministered to them, He ministered to me. I promise you that I am much better off for having put myself aside to do the work of the ministry; although, at the time, it didn't always "feel" like there was any personal growth or gain. The Lord will never allow you or I to "out do" Him. Whatever we give up for His sake or the gospel's, He has promised a recompense of reward (Mark 10:29).

As a choir, we were nowhere near perfection, but we began at least to move in the right direction, and not because I was the "be all" and "end all" or because I did anything special. Whatever I may have done was my reasonable service (Romans 12:1). It was a joint effort of which I was allowed to be a part. That's all. God began to do an individual and a collective work among our members. My part was to understand that my role in the big picture was to be a willing yielded vessel in the Master's Hand, and believe it or not, that brought me tremendous satisfaction and joy.

With this in mind, I remained in place in the choir and continued to minister until the Lord "released" me, which was several years later. I intended to move when the cloud moved as the Israelites did as they journeyed from point A (Egypt) to point B (the Promised Land) (Exodus 13:21). I knew my promotion to the next level that God had for me would be hindered if I had not been sensitive enough to move when He moved.

Furthermore, if I didn't move when God said to move, I could have been occupying a place God assigned to someone else. Thought provoking, isn't it? I might have been hindering another person's promotion by remaining in my position past the appointed time. Again, selfishness rears its ugly head not to mention the fact that I would have been unhappy in a place that had been "reassigned" to someone else. Have you ever been in a position or place where God's anointing has lifted and you are left with frustration and anxiety? You feel "out of sorts." These are pretty good indications that it is time to move on to the next phase or level. Don't hang on to what God is finished with in your life. Relinquish it, and keep moving forward in Him.

One of the things I try to keep in mind is that God may have called me to start something, but He may not have called me to finish it. This is why it is so important to "practice the presence" of His Holy Spirit so you and I can be led at <u>all</u> times.

Eventually, God did release me from the choir and from the ministry. I am grateful to Him for the lessons I learned while I was there. I am grateful for the opportunities He afforded me to develop in the fruit of the Spirit. I can look back now on that time with sincere love and affection for those people. That was the Lord's doing, and it is marvelous in my eyes (Psalm 118:23)!

"For everyone to whom much is given, of him shall much be required; and of him to whom men entrust much, they will require and demand all the more." Luke 12:48

To get a better understanding of this scripture as with any scripture, it is always a good practice to read either the verses that come before or after it or both. In reading several verses before it, you will find that we are encouraged to be "ready" because the Son of Man, Jesus Christ, is coming at an hour and a moment when we do not anticipate it (verse 40). In the simplest of terms, to be "ready" means to ensure that our souls belong to the Lord Jesus Christ by having accepted Him as Lord and as Savior.

The verses that follow compare the return of Jesus to the return of the master of the house who has been away at a marriage feast. In his absence, he has entrusted the responsibility of his household to a steward. The faithful, diligent steward is a wise man who anticipates the return of the master at any given moment, and in the absence of his master, he has carried out his responsibilities. This kind of steward does not require on-site supervision. He simply does what's right, and he does it as unto the Lord.

The verses also compare the good, responsible steward to the irresponsible steward. The irresponsible steward is careless and slothful in his master's absence. He doesn't anticipate a sudden return of the master, and in the interim, he mistreats others and engages in selfish behaviors. Inevitably, the master will return when the steward least expects it, and his irresponsibility will cause unpleasant consequences for him.

This whole scenario parallels our lives as believers in Jesus Christ. If we truly understand our role as Christians, we will understand that we are in the earth to faithfully and responsibly steward or manage those things which the Lord has placed in our care. When I say "things," I am referring to both material and spiritual things. The Bible says every good and perfect gift is from above and comes down from the Father of lights with whom there is no variation or shadow of turning (James 1:17). In other words, all the material gain you and I have amassed, along with the spiritual gifts that have been placed within us, have all come from our Father. We can't lay claim to or take credit for any of them without acknowledging that they have all come from Him.

I believe that one of the concomitants to stewardship is the responsibility of serving people. If we look at Jesus, who is our example in Word and in deed, we will find that He was extremely responsible with His God-given gifts, talents, and abilities. He used them to serve others. In light of the stewardship concept, I decided to do a little self-assessment by asking myself the following questions:

- If Jesus were to return today, what would He find me doing?

- What did God last tell me to do? Am I doing it?

- If I am doing something, is it helping to build the Kingdom of God?

- Why am I doing what I do?

- Am I doing it as unto the Lord with excellence and integrity?

- What am I doing with the gifts God has given me? Am I caring for them properly?

- Are my gifts being used to serve others?

In some cases, my answers to these questions were not what I would have liked them to be, so I chose to self-assess continually in those areas. I wanted to identify those areas that might require adjustments. I had to be careful to avoid allowing selfishness and/or carelessness, with my gifts, to creep into my life. These two can be very subtle, but they will appear without notice nonetheless.

In the midst of this lesson, I learned two very significant things that I would like to share with you. First, don't hold on to anything too tightly because God may ask you to give it away one day. The other is to keep in mind that if God cannot trust you with a little, He will not entrust more to you. For further reading in this area of God's trust in us, refer to the book of Matthew 25, the Parable of the Talents.

I mentioned selfishness and carelessness. Did you know that even though we may purpose in our hearts to do the right thing, we have to bring our flesh into submission to make it happen because the flesh doesn't always want to cooperate? Accepting the responsibility to do what's right even when the right thing is not happening to you can be both challenging and difficult. During these times, our focus has to be on the "big picture," and I have found it necessary to constantly check my attitude while making any necessary adjustments. Sometimes, we will find ourselves doing things we don't want to do, and we'll make sure that everyone around us knows it because of the ugly attitude that might accompany it. Ever been there? Have you ever felt compelled to let others know that you feel like you are doing <u>them</u> a favor? I have. It's not attractive in any way, shape, or form.

It is so vitally important during these challenging times to remember we are here to "serve" not to be served. I can promise you that if we are serving others, God will make sure we are served. The Book of Galatians 6:7-10 tells us:

> Do not be deceived, and deluded and mislead; God will not allow Himself to be sneered at (scorned, disdained, or mocked by mere pretensions or professions, or by His precepts being set aside.) [He inevitably deludes himself who attempts to delude God.] For whatever a man sows, that and that only will he reap. For he who sows to his own flesh (lower nature, sensuality) will from the flesh

reap decay and ruin and destruction, but he who sows to the Spirit will from the Spirit reap eternal life. And let us not lose heart and grow weary and faint in acting nobly and doing right, for in due time and at the appointed season we shall reap, if we do not loosen and relax our courage and faint. So then, as occasion and opportunity open up to us, let us do good [morally] to all people [not only being useful or profitable to them, but also doing what is for their spiritual good and advantage.] Be mindful to be a blessing, especially to those of the household of faith [those who belong to God's family with you, the believers].

When I want to locate myself in the servanthood department, I engage again in self-assessment. Why do I do what I do? Is it for personal gain and/or gratification, or am I doing it to please God? When He becomes the focal point behind the behavior and the attitude, He (the Master) will find you and I doing what's right and maintaining faithfulness over that which has been entrusted to our care. We won't need the Master's constant supervision to stay on the straight and narrow path that leads to life in abundance, to the full, until it overflows in Christ Jesus (John 10:10). God has given us His Word and His Spirit who leads and guides and teaches us into all truth (John 16:13). If I am a "true" believer, then the Word of God is the final authority in my life which settles all matters with all finality.

Sometimes, as human beings, we try to get away with things in the natural when the boss isn't standing right over us. Have you ever surfed the internet or made a personal phone call when the boss wasn't looking? I have. The Lord wants His children to operate in excellence and with integrity, with or without supervision, so that others will know that we are called by His name. Psalm 8:1 tells us His name is excellent in all the earth; therefore, if He is lifted up from the earth [through you and me], He will draw all men to Himself (John 12:32). That's why you are here. That's why I am here. We are to be salt and light in the earth to draw men to the Father (Matthew 5:13-15).

At the most basic level, my job is to help others get saved so they don't have to end up going to hell, dying a second death, where there will be eternal torment. I know this may sound rather hard and harsh, but the Bible is very clear on this outcome if a person's name is not found in the Lamb's Book of Life (Revelation 20:14-15). I don't know about you, but there are a number of people in the world I love very dearly, and I would be sincerely brokenhearted if I had the opportunity to share Jesus Christ with them and didn't take it. Someone shared Him with me. Why would I not want to share Him with someone else?

The other thing, of which we must remain conscious, is that the Master is going to return unexpectedly. The Word says we know neither the day nor the hour when the Son of Man will return. He will come at an hour when we do not expect Him. There will be weeping and gnashing of teeth (Matthew 25:36-51).

Weeping and gnashing of teeth do not sound very attractive to me. I'd just as soon avoid being caught unaware when Jesus comes. Revelation 16:15 further illustrates the point by stating that Jesus is going to come like a thief in the night. Blessed is the man who has remained diligent about his task in his Master's absence. He won't have to worry about being exposed to the shame of not having been a good steward over those things God had given him. Are you a good steward? I plan to continue giving it my very best <u>daily</u> effort.

Life Lessons for Renewing the Mind - Volume I

As believers, you and I cannot afford to be complacent and/or lackadaisical in the work we have been called and assigned to do especially in these "last days." Would you believe that due to some erroneous teaching and thinking, I thought God sat high upon His throne, lightning bolt in hand, just waiting for me to make a mistake so He could strike me with it? I have since learned that that's not the God we serve. He is most assuredly to be reverenced and respected; but at the same time, you and I will never experience from any other human being the kind of love that comes from God. It is forever faithful and matchless. In fact, I will take it one step further by saying that He loves us with the same love that He has shown to His

Son Jesus. We are the apple of His eye (Deuteronomy 32:10) and the beat of His heart. How's that for <u>true</u> love?

It is the Lord's goodness that draws men to repentance (Romans 2:4), and causes us to want to do the right thing. This scripture also tells us we should not allow ourselves to trifle with, through blindness, and presume upon and despise, and underestimate the wealth of His kindness and forbearance and long-suffering patience. I remind myself each day that my Father loves me, and I love Him. Then, as the old folks used to say, I "count my blessings."

How do you love me Lord? Let me count the ways………………………………….. First and foremost, He brought me out of darkness into the marvelous light. He has redeemed my life from death and destruction. He leads and guides me each day by His Holy Spirit. He keeps watch over my family. He supplies all of my needs. He continues to forgive me from sin that is seen and unseen. He's always there and available when I need a friend. I could go on and on about His works and His goodness. Suffice it to say, I am extremely grateful for all that the Lord has done for me. You get the picture.

The point I am trying to make is that I have matured beyond the mental hurdle of committing my life to serving the Lord and His people. I didn't say the task isn't challenging or that I have arrived. Our tasks and assignments will be more challenging when human behavior is involved, but I have resigned myself to the fact that I <u>will</u> go the distance. I will run the race that has been set before me (Hebrews 12:1) for this is my reasonable service.

God has been and continues to be too good to me for me to just sit back and expect to be a receiver and nothing more. Giving is just as wonderful and fulfilling as receiving. I want to serve Him, and in doing so, that involves service to people, even those to whom you might not naturally gravitate. The same goodness God showed me, which drew me to Him, is the same goodness He wants to show through you and me towards other people. Is God awesome, or what?

Life is going to be challenging. Let's keep it real. Dealing with people is no minor and/or easy task, and they are everywhere you go. This is why the Lord has to become the focal point of "why" we do what we do. Keep in mind that just like you and I have had to deal with others, the Lord has to deal with us. Without a doubt, I know that at times, I am no day at the beach. Being human presents challenges for me just like it does for everyone else. That's why I am committed to renewing my mind to the Word of God and allowing His Word to dictate every aspect of both my spiritual and human beings. The Word is the final authority in my life even on the days when I "miss the mark."

God has fully equipped and graced me to fulfill His will for my life. I don't always understand everything, but I am going to continue to trust that He knows what's best for me. With this in mind, He is going to find me faithful over that which He has called me to do and entrusted in my care. I refuse to be caught unaware at the second coming of my Lord and Savior, Jesus Christ, and I purpose in my heart to serve Him all the days of my life. You are invited to join me in this endeavor.

Life Lesson

Did you know that God gives each and every one of us gifts, talents, and abilities? The Word says,

> God's gifts and His call are irrevocable. [He never withdraws them once they are given, and He does not change His mind about those to whom He gives His grace or to whom He sends His call]. (Romans 11:29)

The gifts, talents, and abilities you and I possess have been given to support the will of God for our lives. You might say, "I don't know what the will of God is for my life." If you are anything like I was, I would also add to that statement that initially I didn't even "know" that a will of God existed for me and for every other individual walking the face of the earth.

At the most basic level, His will is for us to love and to serve others. That's how He defines greatness in His Kingdom. In the book of Genesis, Chapter 12, God told Abram he was to go from his father's house to a land that He would show him. There, He would bless him so that he would "be a blessing" to others (1-3). I really want you to meditate on the part of this scripture that states that God would bless Him so that He could <u>bless</u> others. Loving and serving are a part of the "blessing others" concept.

For a very long time, I didn't know I had been born into this earth with a God-given purpose let alone understanding just how that purpose was supposed to translate into a life of servitude. No one ever told me, as a baby Christian, that my job was to "discover" the will of God for my life and then fulfill it. I thank God I know it now and all because of the Word that has been sown into my life by others. Without it, my God-ordained purpose in the earth might have gone unfulfilled.

If I can detach from the spiritual perspective for a moment, I would like to state that even from a humanistic perspective; it would be very frustrating and unfulfilling for anyone to have lived a life without purpose. I want to leave a legacy behind. How about you? For what will you be remembered?

As I began to mature spiritually, I started learning some things about the will of God for my life. In the process of gaining a better understanding, I found myself wanting to know "why" I had been put on this earth "for such a time as this" (Esther 4:14). I began to read books about how to discover the will of God for my life. I also read books that helped to pinpoint my strengths and areas of passion. These kinds of tools helped to keep me motivated and moving forward in my pursuit of God's perfect will for me. As a matter of fact, I still read these kinds of books. I have become more knowledgeable about His will, but I certainly have not arrived. I just keep moving forward in Him every day to the best of my ability.

If you have not taken the time, I would encourage you to go to your local Christian book store and begin to read through some of the titles that refer to discovering the will of God for your life. There are any number of spiritual leaders who have written these types of books to "train up" the Body of Christ. Pick one that appeals to you, and get started. If there are videotapes and/or CDs available, I would encourage you to get them as well. Watch and listen to them over and over to the point of saturation. Each time you play them, you are not only taking the opportunity to mature in your spirit, but they will give you an opportunity to meditate in the Word. Listen for the voice of the Lord.

While I was interacting with these kinds of materials, my prayers began to include petitions asking the Lord to show me the direction in which He would have me to go. During the process, I had to learn to start stepping out in faith at His urging or unction. Allow me to clarify that my "stepping out" required an appropriate corresponding action to my faith.

Faith is not limited to our confessions. Without works, it is dead (James 2:17), which means we have to make a start somewhere. If we will just start, God will help us. He will meet us right where we are.

I recall a believer saying that when God told her it was time to step out, she told Him that she would go, if He would show her "where" to go. There was nothing wrong with her request, but God was giving her a chance to step out in faith. He told her that He would show her, _if_ she went. That was an important "if" that would have an impact on her life forever.

Stepping out before you "know" requires faith. The testimony that I just shared describes me accurately. I have always wanted to see the big picture at the outset. In other words, I wanted a full set of blueprints from the Lord in order to "make a move." What I discovered was that I would have no need for faith, if I knew everything upfront. If the truth were to be told, I feared missing God, and in many instances, it held me back from the active or behavioral component of my faith. I didn't know that sometimes you have to "miss it" to "make it." Thank God that He finds us no matter what detour we've taken in pursuit of obedience, and He redirects our steps back towards the right path.

A wonderful byproduct of this "stepping out" and moving forward process is that our faith and trust in God begin to build and take shape. We begin to become more familiar with His voice. We discover how to discern what is or isn't God. One way to determine the origin of a voice is to line up what you've heard with the Word of God. God always speaks in line with His written Word. If it doesn't line up with the Word of God, then it isn't God.

Walking with God is going to require ongoing, "never say die no matter what it looks like" faith. Needless to say, the Lord is still working with me, but isn't it extremely comforting to know He is so wonderfully patient? I can rest knowing He will continue to work with me, even through my mistakes, until He gets me to the next level. If you know anything about God, you know that He is always encouraging His children to go higher in Him. He doesn't ever want us to sit back on our laurels with an "I've arrived" attitude. There are always higher heights and deeper depths to discover in Him. He is, without a doubt, unfathomable.

While I was learning to trust God during my faith walk, I lost sight of the fact that He is the author and the finisher of my faith (Hebrews 12:2). What does that mean? The amplified version of this scripture explains that Jesus gave the first incentive for our belief, and that He will bring it to maturity and perfection. These things will not come unless you and I have a willingness to trust God and walk by faith and not by sight (2 Corinthians 5:7).

The first part of Hebrews 12:2 tells us to look away from all that will distract and look to Jesus. This includes looking away from the fear while casting down those thoughts that are contrary to the Word of God, the not knowing, the concerns about being on the wrong road, the concerns about not having the blueprint, the concerns about making mistakes, etc. You get my point. These are distractions, and God wants us to focus on Jesus so He can mature and perfect our faith.

Once I settled it in my heart and mind that I was going to be the kind of woman who possesses the faith that pleases God (Hebrews 11:6), I was ready to continue in my search for the will of God for my life. As I stated earlier, I had read a number of books on this topic as well as having heard a number of good teaching messages. I was out of the starting blocks and on my way. I began to acknowledge and receive the gifts, talents, and abilities God had given me. By stepping out in various areas, I found out immediately, in some cases, whether or not I was called to do that particular thing.

Another very helpful attempt in discovering the will of God for my life was taking a very serious inventory of my life. What I mean is that I took the time to reflect about where I was in my life. How had I arrived at that point? I began to ask myself about and identify the kinds of things towards which I tended to gravitate. What were my likes and dislikes as a child? As an adult? When did I feel most fulfilled? For what did I have a passion? These kinds of questions helped me to hone in on the gifts God has given me.

Life Lessons for Renewing the Mind - Volume I

I don't mind sharing with you that this book is an outgrowth of the discovery that I have a sincere God-given desire to help people. As my relationship with the Lord has matured, this desire has become even stronger. I can remember even as a child that I was always in the position of playing the advocate for others. I always gravitated towards the underdog and attempted to do what I could to help that person. When I got older, I increased what I could do because I had more resources at my disposal. I had been blessed to be a blessing. Even then, God was touching my heart with empathy for someone else's infirmity, but I had not recognized it as such.

Now, I consistently pray to maintain a sincere compassion for others. I understand it was that <u>same</u> compassion the Father showed me by allowing Jesus to die on the cross (John 3:16). Jesus died for me when I was still "dead in my sins," and He continued to wait for me to "get a clue" about needing to receive Him as my Savior. He overlooked the fact that I continued to reject Him because He saw Kingdom potential in me. He sees it in you. Knowing this makes me extremely grateful to my Heavenly Father. It also compels me to want to be obedient and to serve Him with a heart of gratitude. Whatever He tells me to do, I am going to do it (John 2:5) to the best of my natural ability.

In my prayer time, God ministered something to me that I think is very profound, and I have always remembered it. He said, "Just as your life depended upon Jesus' obedience, someone else's life depends upon your obedience." Wow! With this in mind, I can't afford to be disobedient or do what God has called me to do with a halfhearted effort. God has not saved me for me. He has saved me, renewed my mind, gifted me, matured me etc., to help someone else, which is why none of us can afford to be selfish and/or self-centered, if we are calling ourselves Christians. At the end of the day, it's not about you or me. It's about building the Kingdom of God.

Each and every one of the Lord's children has the same commission, and it is to go into all the world and preach the good news of the gospel of Jesus Christ (Mark 16:15). In other words, tell others about the goodness of God through His Son, Jesus, and what His death on the cross has purchased for each us.

Share with them what great and marvelous things He has done for you personally, and if the opportunity presents itself, lead him or her to Christ. A simple prayer of salvation appears in the back of the book that can be used if you're not sure what to say. Talking to God in prayer can be as simple and as uncomplicated as conversing with your best friend. Are you a friend of God? God called Abraham friend.

I am Abraham's seed; therefore, I too am a friend of God (James 2:22-24).

By no means do I want to give the impression that I am completely "in the know" about the will of God for my life. I am not sitting back with my hands behind my head and my feet up with a list where I have written all these things down just waiting for them to unfold and manifest in my life so that I can check them off. I have continued my search in the area of the will of God for my life, and I am grateful to God that I am farther along than I was at the outset.

Rather than being sort of "all over the place," I have discovered that my skill set seems to be culminating somehow in particular areas. I don't quite know how to describe it, but God is refining them and making the big picture clearer to me. I have always had the pieces, but initially I didn't know it. Time and the leadership of the Holy Spirit have been required for discovery and maturation in this area. "It is the glory of God to conceal a thing; but the glory of kings is to search out a thing" (Proverbs 25:2).

Another thing I have come to understand is that God has been preparing me to do His will all this time through my experiences, my education, through people, and His Word. Did you know He doesn't waste any of these things? What I mean is that you, like me, may have thought you were pursuing something or going through something for one reason, but God may have had a completely different agenda in mind. Hindsight, sometimes, will reveal this to you.

For me, there have been many times when I simply have not understood what was going on, but hindsight stepped in to provide me with some understanding. I found out when I looked at the situation a little more closely, I discovered that God was present and working in my life all along. When I am able to "see" this, I am able to thank Him for what He did in the situation, even though I may not have understood at the time why it was happening. With maturation, I have been able to thank Him without any sight at all.

Would you believe that God has also brought me to the point where I can actually thank Him for adverse situations? I never thought it to be possible. It boggles my mind sometimes because as human beings we have a tendency to shy away from those things that will cause pain or discomfort in our lives. We want to avoid these kinds of things at all costs, but God has promised that He will never leave us nor forsake us (Hebrews 13:5). Further assurance in God's concern for us is stated in Psalm 34:19, "Many are the afflictions of the righteous, but God delivers him out of them all." Understand that afflictions are going to come to the people of God, but He doesn't just deliver us out of one test, trial, or tribulation. He delivers us out of them <u>all</u>. Besides, we have to have the challenges to help us to grow and mature in Him.

Preparation is paramount in walking out the will of God for your life. I didn't know it then, but I know it now. I can remember feeling like there were a number of gifts that still needed to be developed in my life. They seemed burdensome and unmanageable, if that makes sense. I used to ask God about why I seemed to have more than my share, if you will, of gifts. One of the answers He gave me was that I answered the call when He called.

The Bible says that many are called, but few are chosen (Matthew 20:16). In other words, people have and will be given the opportunity to serve the Lord.

Many will have an opportunity to answer the call, but it will only be answered by those who are willing to accept the responsibility for that call upon their lives. God loves people. We are His creation, and He is extremely serious about our souls, which means if He takes it seriously, so should we.

With this in mind, I recall once again what He said to me in my prayer time, "Just as your life depended upon Jesus' obedience, someone else's life is dependent upon your obedience." We, who are willing to accept the responsibility for the call, must then understand that someone else's life is on the line, sometimes literally.

It's "time out" for playing around with the lives of God's people. God is looking for those who will see, through the eyes of Jesus, that people are precious and that He doesn't throw them away. People throw people away. To help you and me in the "people endeavor," He makes an investment in our lives through many of the things I mentioned earlier, and He expects a return on His investment. I need to clarify that His, and I emphasize His not ours, return on His investment should not be a self-serving one. We should never entertain a mindset where we think we have "arrived" and have been given a license to look down upon others in disdain who may not be where we are. God's investment in you and me should yield some serious "let's stop playing, and get this thing right" Kingdom building.

When you get right down to it, isn't that why we are here? If it isn't, why bother? What can be any more important than accepting the awesome responsibility God offers each and every one of us everyday to assist in building up His Kingdom? As far as I am concerned, it just doesn't get any better than that. I dare you to try to find any undertaking that is more satisfying or rewarding than the one "offered" to us by our Father. It's an offer, I cannot and will not refuse. How about you?

I have decided to receive the gifts God has given me along with the call upon my life, but I must remember that to whom much is given, from him much will be required (Luke 12:48). I challenge you to think about what have you decided to do for God. Can He count on you? You may feel like you either don't have an assignment from God, or you don't know what your assignment is. The Bible says that we have not because we ask not (James 4:2). Ask God to show you the assignment He has for you. If the assignment has fallen by the wayside, pick it up, and ask Him to revive you. Get reassigned!

Remember that your specific assignment was chosen for you before the foundation of the world. God doesn't have to sit and think up something to give you now that you have decided to ask Him for it, perhaps even for the one-hundredth time. With God, it's very simple. As He reveals your assignment, I encourage you to receive it with the respect and the responsibility that it deserves, but most of all, receive it with joy. I promise you there will never be anything in your life that will bring you more joy and satisfaction than fulfilling the will of God for your life.

Prayer of Salvation

Father I come to You, in the name of Jesus, acknowledging that I need you as Lord and Savior of my life. Your Word says that if I confess with my mouth that Jesus is Lord and believe in my heart You raised Him from the dead, I shall be saved. Jesus, come into my heart right now. I declare that You are Lord over my life!

Lord I thank you that from this day forward, my name is written in the Lamb's Book of Life because of the quality decision I have made today. I set my will right now to forgive those that have hurt me for I know that forgiveness is the manner of the Kingdom of God, and offense is the seed of unforgiveness; therefore, I refuse to be offended. I refuse to plant that seed in my heart. I release those who have hurt me right now in the name of Jesus.

I thank You Lord for my new life in Christ. Thank you that old things are passed away, and that you have made me a new creature regardless of what I think, what I feel, or what others might say. As I begin my walk with You Lord, I thank You that You will raise up people to help me become all that you have created me to be.

Holy Spirit, I invite You into the driver's seat of my life. I declare and decree that I will have a purpose driven life. I thank You in advance that You will lead me, guide me, and teach me each day into all truths. In Jesus' mighty name, I pray with thanksgiving, Amen!

If you have prayed this prayer of salvation, know that Jesus has come into your heart <u>immediately.</u> Allow me to be the first to welcome you into the Kingdom my brother or my sister. Welcome to the Family!

Sometimes, a change in season can be the catalyst for the start of something new in your life. Keep moving forward from the old mind sets to the new minds sets in God. Meditate on the Word of God day and night, that you may observe and do according to all that is written in it. For then you shall make your way prosperous, and then you shall deal wisely and have good success (Joshua 1:8).